Contents

Editorial

This collection of articles aims to identify a few of the many issues that are critical for women — and men — today, and that look likely to remain so for the next ten or 20 years. It recalls why the project of promoting gender-equitable development continues to be critical in the twenty-first century; identifies some key challenges which face those working on gender and development in this rapidly changing field; and takes a brief look at some examples of innovative work.

The key themes in this collection are globalisation and diversity. Globalisation is an issue for gender and development work because of its sheer scale, and the far-reaching implications it has for the lives of women and men living in poverty. It offers a challenge to development researchers and workers who seek to analyse, address, and ultimately eradicate human poverty and marginalisation. How can they respond to poverty in a world where financial deals are made in seconds on the internet, where governments are powerless in the face of international trade flows and economic policies, and where transnational corporations can move their operations freely around the world? How can development workers understand social marginalisation in the context of world cities where McDonald's outlets are located beside shanty towns, and trafficked sex workers and international financiers increasingly coexist within a few metres of each other?

The concepts of difference and diversity — of individual identity, experience, and attitude — invite us to narrow our focus to the particular, in order to understand the world at the start of the twenty-first century. People all experience poverty differently. Over the past two decades, this simple fact has become more recognised in development debates, and many of the concepts and assumptions that were common currency in the twentieth-century context of colonialism and its aftermath have been called into question. In a globalised world, crude models of Northern/ Western, rich, industrialised countries on the one hand, and Southern, poor, 'developing' countries on the other, must finally be laid to rest. This vigorous questioning of stereotypes of poverty and marginalisation is familiar to gender and development (GAD) workers, who have seen similar challenges mounted by Southern activists and researchers against racist caricatures of 'poor Southern women' and assumptions that a strong women's movement is led from the North/West (Mohanty 1988).

Globalisation has been associated with human exploitation and environmental degradation, as well as the creation of new opportunities. This collection begins with a group of articles examining economic, political, and social changes associated with globalisation, and analysing their positive and negative impacts on different women and men. In a globalised economy, with its concomitant political and social change, development policy-makers and practitioners need more urgently than ever to understand the very different impact of international macroeconomic policies on individual women and men within the household, community, region, and state. The current processes of globalisation need to be seen in the context of earlier global processes of wealth-creation and impoverishment, including colonialism. It is these processes which have led to the current gender- and race-biased patterns of marginalisation and poverty throughout the world, and which are a significant factor in people's ability to respond to global change today.

The articles here trace the ways in which specific aspects of globalisation affect gender relations, and shape women's and men's choices and chances. In particular, writers highlight the failure of governments and development agencies to challenge fully the false assumptions about the nature of women's and men's roles in society upon which global economic activity is based. They have yet to move beyond verbal acknowledgements of the worth of unpaid reproductive work, or to develop policies that enable women to share the burden of caring with men and the state (Folbre 1994). Until this happens, women face structural and cultural barriers to taking advantage of the economic and political changes associated with globalisation.

How can gender and development researchers, practitioners, and policy-makers respond to women's and men's poverty and marginalisation, now and in the future? A second group of articles invites us to revisit the basic concepts and terminology used in gender and development work, and to enrich them by taking on insights from academic research, as well as feedback from practitioners. We must re-evaluate our analytical tools and concepts of gender analysis and our professional practice, in order to develop the mature understanding of development, poverty, and marginalisation that we need. How can our tools be sharpened, so that they take into account the widely varying experiences of different women — and men — living in the same global context? Failure to ask these questions may lead us to misunderstand how to address gender inequality. We need to recognise that gender discrimination is interlinked with other factors of social differentiation, and that men's lives, like women's, are shaped by gender issues.

Finally, where do we look for new ways forward? The third group of articles in this collection offers innovative, interesting case studies of current gender-sensitive development work. Writers focus on topical issues, including acknowledging sexuality as a development issue, critiquing the assumption of entrepreneurship as gender-neutral, and asserting the need for mainstream institutions, including government and development funders, to work with women's organisations. Here, too, diversity is a key concern.

What is globalisation?

Globalisation was defined in 1996 as 'a process whereby producers and investors increasingly behave as if the world economy consisted of a single market and production area with regional or national sub-sectors, rather than a set of national economies linked by trade and investment flows' (UN 1996, 6). While transnational corporations and international financial institutions have stressed the benefits of globalisation for human development, others see the process as an enforced opening-up of fragile developing country markets for the benefit of the post-industrial world: 'the integration of the powerless marginal third world into the agenda set by the West' (Afshar and Barrientos 1999, 2, citing Dijaba 1997).

In her article, Ruth Pearson discusses the implications of economic globalisation for the daily lives, and the status, of women, tracing the ways in which this process has affected the relationship between women and men positioned in different locations. 'The markets in today's global system are creating wonderful opportunities, but distributing them unevenly' (UNDP 1999, 84). As Pearson stresses, the ability to grasp the best opportunities is determined by women's and men's different degrees of freedom to take on waged employment, and of skills and training, including literacy. Women (and men) who have responsibilities for unpaid reproductive work fail on the first of these criteria; in developing countries, women are also disproportionately likely to be uneducated and illiterate. These barriers result in the feminisation of poverty.

In their article, Carol Barton and Elmira Nazombe present anecdotes of women's lives in developing and post-industrial countries which illustrate the common roots of women's ostensibly different problems in a globalised economy. Women in post-industrialised, industrialising and non-industrial settings are obliged to take on most of the work of reproducing the human race. This work is unrecognised in a global economic system which is based on assumptions of paid work as the only work with economic value, perpetuating the fatigue of women condemned to work a double day. As the UNDP points out, 'markets can go too far and squeeze the non-market activities so critical for human development. Because of a *fiscal squeeze*, the public provision of social services is being constrained. Because of a *time squeeze*, the personal provision of (unpaid) caring services is being reduced' (UNDP 1999, 84). As a result of this continuing and wilful blindness to the 'structural constraints' on women caring for dependents (Folbre 1994), women's inclusion in paid employment is not likely to be on terms of their choosing: they will earn less than men for similar jobs; jobs considered 'women's work' will be in markets where pay is lower; and their conditions of employment may be exploitative on many counts.

Colletah Chitsike points out in her article that — despite nearly three decades of 'mainstreaming' gender into development — planners still disregard these structural constraints on women producers, and also fail to recognise cultural sanctions against them. Her article presents a critique of the current vogue for projects promoting women's entrepreneurship, which are being transferred to diverse communities across the world, in post-industrial, developing, and post-communist countries. In much of this work, the basic insights of gender analysis are forgotten.

Looking at the global level and discussing the opportunities open to *some* in a globalised world should not lead to amnesia or apathy about absolute poverty. In her article, Fra von Massow discusses health and education research initiated by Oxfam in Ethiopia, the world's third poorest country (UNDP 1999). Von Massow's article provides a 'reality check' for anyone who may have forgotten that in 2000, there are communities so acutely poor and marginalised by resource-providers that not a single woman has access to trained health-care attendants when giving birth. This 0 per cent access rate in Ethiopia must be seen against a background of environmental degradation, chronic malnutrition, a government which spends money on a war that it cannot afford, and relative to a growing sense among the communities that, as one Ethiopian woman describes it, they are 'forgotten on earth' (von Massow, this issue). In a population already facing acute poverty, women are marginalised from decision-making; expected to marry young; and to leave their reproductive destiny to fate. The aim of health for all by 2015 has no reality in such a context.

Worldwide, there are many thousands of women and men like those speaking in von Massow's research: excluded from the potential benefits of globalisation, living in remote, usually rural, areas with few forms of communication (be they roads and transport, or access to the internet). However isolated they may seem, though, the impact of global policies — for example, on debt repayment, the environment, and political stability — has a direct and devastating effect on these communities' lives.

Women's empowerment, democracy, and governance

The process of globalisation of the economy — now advanced to the extent that some refer to it as a condition (Panos 1999) — has clear implications for the role of governments in states and regional political and economic federations. Globalisation is often characterised as undermining governments' powers to legislate to protect their populations' welfare. Two articles in this collection address this point, in very different ways.

In her article on the complex linkages between globalisation, democracy, and women's empowerment, Sylvia Walby states, 'Globalisation has often been represented as a process which is hostile to democracy, yet globalisation and democratisation have been taking place at the same time ... sometimes feminist pessimism about contemporary developments can go too far' (Walby, this issue). It is true, in many situations, that the power of transnational corporations (TNCs) and foreign investors to determine employment levels and working conditions now exceeds that of national governments. However, national governments — even democratic ones — have a patchy record of including women in governance, or progressing their rights through policy. Both Walby and Pearson assert that globalisation can offer women and other marginalised groups unprecedented opportunities to transcend national politics and create pressure groups that will ultimately transform them. In particular, global communications technologies have enabled the dynamic and hugely influential international women's movement to pioneer an innovative and very successful global advocacy campaign, targeting, but also going beyond, the series of UN conferences in the 1990s.

Challenges to political systems posed by economic globalisation are matched by its challenge to the distinct social and cultural life of different parts of the world, as globalised production depends on stimulating global demand for consumer goods. The role of the media is central in promoting stereotyped views of women simultaneously as sex objects and home-makers, to promote the sale of newspapers and raise viewing figures for television programmes, as well as seemingly endless arrays of related consumer disposables. The Fourth UN Women's Conference in Beijing in 1995 called on the media to reform themselves as a step towards promoting a global culture in which women are recognised as full human beings, and their economic, political, and social rights enforced (http://www.un.org/womenwatch/daw/beijing/platform). Pat Made, a journalist from Zimbabwe, discusses the efforts of her organisation to respond to this call by introducing gender-awareness training for its journalists throughout the world.

Balancing local and global realities

In the first of a group of articles exploring possible responses to global change on the part of gender and development policy-makers and practitioners, Judy El-Bushra invites us to sharpen the basic conceptual tools we use in GAD, to ensure that they serve us well in understanding the cross-cutting factors of disadvantage — including gender, race, class, and caste — which together cause poverty and social exclusion. Drawing on her experience of gender and development work in various African contexts, she highlights issues which will be familiar to many. The reality of poverty and marginalisation faced by individual women (and men) is very different according to the context, and local realities may deviate enormously from the picture painted by global statistics. Over the past decade, there has been a move away from blanket acceptance that women, as a category, always have it worse than men, to a realisation that factors including class, caste, and race are as important as gender in determining social differentiation, and the way women and men see themselves. We know from the history of twentieth-century national liberation struggles in various countries (including South Africa, Nicaragua, and Eritrea) that at various points in their lives, individuals will see a particular part of their identity as the determining one, and that these perceptions alter over the course of a lifetime.

Recognising sexuality as central to development

In general, human sexuality has been a challenging area for development organisations. In particular, stereotypical views of female sexuality as powerless and passive, and a lack of awareness of the ways in which sexuality is linked to economic concerns in the institution of the family, have hampered policy-makers seeking to promote women's reproductive rights and to prevent the spread of HIV and other sexually transmitted diseases. Judy El-Bushra argues that, in future, GAD researchers and workers will have to consider how to adapt our understanding of gender as a concept to take in new insights about sex, sexuality, and gender, from scientific and social research. Anthropologists, natural scientists, and social scientists are currently questioning the clear concepts of sex and gender (Oakley 1972) on which we have based our gender training and planning for more than 20 years. This requires us to engage with ideas which are often alien, and sometimes threatening to the world-view which we have been brought up to consider the norm. However, since those of us involved in gender work daily ask men and women to recognise the social origin of much they previously viewed as natural, we should surely be prepared to question our own assumptions.

The first development planners to consider the centrality of sexuality to human development worked on the issue of population, but by the 1980s, many had rejected population control policies in favour of promoting women's empower-ment to accept contraception, through a focus on female education and employment (Bown 1990). In 1994, at the UN Conference on Population and Development in Cairo, the women's movement argued that most women are not free to determine who their sexual partners are, or when, where, and how they have sex.

In her article on sex workers' responses to HIV prevention in Calcutta, Madhu Bala Nath discusses a highly participatory intervention run by sex workers for sex workers, which is based on peer education: not only about the mechanics of disease prevention, but about the structural nature of women's subordination, which in many situations renders them powerless to negotiate about sex or make decisions about child-bearing. Women who resist male control risk violent reprisals. The Calcutta sex workers have since become involved in national and international groups which assert women's right to earn a living in any way they choose, which reject double standards that demonise sex workers and eulogise marriage (the site of subordination for many women), and which understand sex work as a dignified and resourceful response to overcoming poverty. A key lesson from Madhu Bala Nath's article is that alliances can be built between unlikely groups of people if the need to do so is overwhelming. Sex workers in Calcutta have worked in a pragmatic manner to gain the support of regular clients, the police, and even some pimps, for the use of condoms.

Building alliances

In his article, Peter Sternberg makes a case for gender and development work with men as a target group, as a key to reproductive health. He discusses the experience of the Centro de Información y Servicios de Asesoría en Salud (CISAS), a Nicaraguan NGO, in health promotion with men. Through action-research workshops that encourage men to consider their views on parenting, sexuality, and *machismo*, CISAS aims to help men take responsibility for their actions. A growing men's movement is currently asserting what the women's movement has said for years: that men are gendered beings, not a 'norm' from which women deviate, and that they therefore face particular issues associated with their masculine identity and role.

As Sternberg argues, projects focusing on men must be founded on a gender analysis of unequal power relations between women and men, and go hand-in-hand with complementary policies and interventions which promote women's inalienable right to the final say in reproductive decision-making. If they do

this, they may be extremely useful to humanity. Certainly, it is clear that attaining equality for women needs attention to resistance on the part of the 'other half' (White 1994, 98); it is also clear that individual men may find that the cost of being a man in their context may be higher than the 'patriarchal dividend'[1] that all men can draw on. However, in the absence of any commitment to changing gender relations, interventions which focus on promoting men's decision-making in reproductive matters are essentially retrogressive, reinforcing rather than challenging oppressive gender relations.

Over the next five years, it will be fascinating to see whether development organisations, including NGOs, will be faster to embrace the ideas of the men's movement than they have been in the past three decades to build alliances with the women's movement. Those of us in mainstream development-funding agencies know that, at best, strong alliances between mainstream organisations and the women's movement have eventually been forged, leading to joint projects which transform gender relations and eradicate poverty. At worst, women's organisations are rejected as partners, caricatured variously as extremist and therefore too threatening to work with, or as elitist and out of touch with the 'grassroots women' with whom development organisations wish to work.

One challenge to the dominant view of sex and gender in our work argues that they are based on an assumption that all societies have two clear gender identities which 'match' two sexes. Ultimately, this means that GAD work does not challenge prejudice against same-sex sexualities, and, by its acceptance of clear norms of bodies and behaviour, betrays those who do not fall into these categories. As Susie Jolly shows in her article, denial of human rights of lesbians and gay men is an issue not only for human rights activists, but for development workers, in both South and

North. The issue of same-sex sexualities is most commonly taken on by anti-HIV and reproductive health interventions; but there are many other areas of development where programming needs to change. In particular, lesbians are forced to choose between their bodily integrity and their economic security in societies where women do not have full legal majority and must marry in order to gain access to assets and resources, for example, land.

As Susie Jolly points out in her article, homosexuality is often seen as a Western phenomenon; in fact, the desire of a sizeable minority to have sexual relationships with the same sex is present throughout the world. Tolerance of difference and diversity is critical for peaceful human development, and GAD workers in particular have as a resource the long experience of the women's movement in learning not only to cope with diversity, but to recognise it as a strength.

Conclusion

After the first 25 years of WID and GAD work in international and national development institutions, aiming to eradicate women's poverty and marginalisation, what has been achieved? From their divers perspectives, articles in this collection argue compellingly that the work of redressing gender inequality has only just begun. On the economic front, women are still disproportionately likely to be poor: global statistics are a clear testament to the work which has yet to be done. As UNIFEM states: 'Women are still the poorest of the world's poor, representing 70 percent of the 1.3 billion people who live in absolute poverty. When nearly 900 million women have incomes of less than $1 a day, the association between gender inequality and poverty remains a harrowing reality' (http://www.undp.org/unifem/economic. htm). In politics and decision-making at all levels of society, women's voices are muted or silent. Global estimates of the incidence

of violence against women bear witness to men's freedom to abuse women who they perceive to be challenging male authority, with minimal risk of punishment. The World Health Organisation estimates that at least one in five women have been physically or sexually abused by a man at some time in their lives (WHO 1997).

How can these statistics be related to the assertions of governments and other service-providers that they are taking a 'more strategic approach ... which promotes full equality between women and men in all spheres of life, addressing the causes as well as the consequences of inequality and aiming to bring about fundamental changes in gender relations' (DfID 1998, 1)? Siobhan Riordan argues in her article that this approach is not being taken in the UK, or in the context of development. Repeated studies of the ways in which gender issues 'evaporate' from our organisations bear witness to the difficulty of turning rhetoric about power and social transformation into action. In general, the non-economic aspects of the feminist agenda have been paid lip-service only. 'It is widely recognised that the concepts of "gender and development" and "women in development" have frequently been construed as one and the same thing, and often not mistakenly' (Chant 2000, forthcoming). In Riordan's research in the UK, she found chronic under-funding of gender-equality initiatives, both in mainstream institutions (including government) and in funding disbursed to women's organisations. Riordan points out that the very existence of the women's movement bears witness to women's need to meet their own concerns, and the failure of governments and mainstream NGOs to do so. While transformative work to address gender power relations may be carried out on a small scale, global powers — including the international financial institutions, the UN and other bodies — are lagging behind.

The articles included here demonstrate not only the importance of understanding how individuals react and respond to global policies according to their identity and location, but the iterative relationship between people's *chances* (which are shaped by their economic, political and social surroundings, including gender relations) and their *choices* (in terms of the way they exercise their agency to conform, resist or transform their surroundings). Throughout history, women and men have overcome and circumvented obstacles to move forward, and this will continue in future. Funding and support is needed from mainstream institutions at the international level to facilitate the efforts of all those women, and men, who wish to transform human life for the better by bringing about fundamental changes to gender relations.

Note

1 The 'patriarchal dividend' refers to the fact that even if an individual man chooses to reject exercising power over women, he benefits from the existence of male-biased structures and institutions which will discriminate in his favour (Connell 1995).

References

Bown L (1990) *Preparing the Future: Women, literacy and development*, Action Aid, London.

Connell RW (1995) *Masculinities*, Blackwell, UK.

Department for International Development (1998) *Breaking the Barriers: Women and the elimination of world poverty*, DfID, London.

Mohanty C (1988) 'Under Western eyes: feminist scholarship and colonial discourses', in *Feminist Review*, 30.

Oakley (1972) *Sex, Gender and Society*, Temple Smith.

UN (1996) *Globalisation and Liberalisation: Development in the face of two powerful currents*, report of the Secretary-General to the ninth session of the UN Conference on Trade and Development, UN, New York and Geneva.

White S (1994) 'Making men an issue: Gender planning for "the other half"', in Macdonald M (ed) *Gender Planning in Development Agencies: Meeting the challenge*, Oxfam GB, Oxford.

Moving the goalposts:
Gender and globalisation in the twenty-first century

Ruth Pearson

Development institutions saw their work challenged by those working on gender and development in the last third of the twentieth century. Ruth Pearson argues that the new century will witness an assertion of the global relevance of gender in development, and see gender analysis applied in new contexts, and to men as well as women.

Talk of globalisation is all the rage at the beginning of the new millennium. Some see it as the beginning of a new era which promises integration and development for all, with technology, investment, and trade overcoming geographical and economic isolation. Others understand globalisation as the acceleration of an on-going process of economic polarisation, in which more 'developed' regions get richer and richer, while countries in the periphery (particularly in sub-Saharan Africa, most of Latin America, parts of south and south-east Asia, and the former Soviet Union) become further impoverished and politically unstable, with little prospect of catching up and developing alongside the more prosperous parts of the world.[1]

Certain phenomena — including the HIV/AIDS pandemic, environmental degradation, pollution, global warming, civil and national conflict and insecurity — affect people throughout the world. It is also clear that the ability of individual states to challenge the larger forces emanating from beyond their frontiers is diminishing, and people from poorer and less developed regions are particularly vulnerable.

What does globalisation mean?

Globalisation is a term that has a broad and elastic meaning, denoting the process in which economic, financial, technical, and cultural transactions between different countries and communities throughout the world are increasingly interconnected, and embody common elements of experience, practice, and understanding.

However, many commentators focus only on the economic aspects of globalisation. For instance, the Secretary-General of UNCTAD defined it as 'a process whereby producers and investors increasingly behave as if the world economy consisted of a single market area with regional or national sub-sectors, rather than a set of national economies linked by trade and investment flows' (UNCTAD 1996, 6, cited in Panos 1999).

This focus on the economic aspect of globalisation reflects the extraordinary concentration of international trade, investment, and financial flows in recent years. There are many indicators of this: for example, foreign direct investment in production facilities has expanded twenty-fold in recent decades, from US$21.5 billion in 1973, to US$400 billion in 1997 (Panos 1999, 2). Transnational corporations (among the main instruments of globalisation of production) are now responsible for 80 per cent of foreign direct investment, and directly employ up to 50 million people in Export Processing Zones throughout the world (ibid.). Although this is only a fraction of the world's workforce, together with sub-contractors and allied services it represents a sizeable, and increasing, proportion of global employment and production.

Globalisation of trade and investment has also been accompanied by a rapid growth in financial flows across national borders for investment and speculation in commodities including financial products and currencies. The integration of world financial markets has become a very significant feature of the modern world economy. The Asian financial crisis in 1997/8, which started in Thailand and spread to Malaysia, Indonesia, and Japan, revealed the extent to which national economies and financial systems are interlinked one with another. On another side of the world, rather than cut off financial assistance to Russia in the face of the chronic instability of its economy, the World Bank and the IMF have offered additional short- and medium-term financial assistance in order to prevent financial crisis spreading to other parts of an increasingly interdependent world economy.

Technological change, associated with the so-called 'third industrial revolution'[2] has been at the heart of many changes in the world economy. The first of these is the ability of international corporations to operate on a scale that increasingly transcends national and regional borders. The scale and range of international transactions would not have been possible without the technology of electronic transfer and calculation of transactions. New technology has made possible the co-ordination of production and trade internationally, often from metropolitan centres, so that locally based sectors such as

fruit, flowers, and vegetable production are now co-ordinated on a global scale to serve markets all over the world. Second, the production of the semi-conductor (micro-chip) and its applications in computers and telecommunications have had significant effects on global trade and production. A range of new electronics components and equipment for military, production, and consumption markets, are now being developed and marketed in different parts of the world. Third, new computer and tele-communications technologies including the worldwide web have facilitated the spread of a whole range of new services and processes such as data entry, e-commerce, consumer-service call centres, and enter-tainment and leisure services, implying that neither production nor consumption of these services need be constrained by geographical boundaries or distance.

A key aspect of globalisation which is associated with these widespread economic and technical changes is the well-marked trend of international and national movements of populations. These have resulted not merely in growing urbanisation, but specifically in the creation of 'world cities' (Sassen 1991), starting with the global financial centres of New York, London, and Tokyo, followed by Paris, Frankfurt, Zurich, Amsterdam, Los Angeles, Sydney, and Hong Kong, and now including the 'mega-conurbations' of Mexico City, San Paolo, Buenos Aires, Bangkok, Tapai, and Bombay (Sassen 1998)[3].

The existence of these cities — literally 'concrete' manifestations of globalisation — reflects another very significant aspect of the contemporary world, that of increasing inequalities. Over the past 20 years, the share of income received by the poorest fifth of the world's population has dropped (from 2.3 per cent to 1.4 per cent), while the proportion taken by the richest fifth has risen. By the mid 1990s, in sub-Saharan Africa 20 countries had lower incomes per head in real terms than they had in the late

1970s (Giddens 1999). Within global cities, the same kind of inequalities coexist: the rich and well educated have lifestyles that reflect the advantages of global growth. Large numbers of low-paid workers — many of whom are migrants from poorer countries and regions — produce high-quality goods for consumption by their high-living neighbours, while others provide personal services for them.

As well as the diminishing spatial segregation between rich and poor, and the growth of metropolitan and peripheral communities, a combination of global communications technology, and marketing and advertising techniques have produced global patterns of consumption and tastes. These are transcending local customs and resource allocations. For example, the universal demand for certain kinds of sports and leisure wear — Nike trainers or Levi's jeans, or 'fast' or 'convenience' foods such as McDonald's hamburgers and Nestlé baby milk — is created by global practices rather than local priorities. The creation of global demand for such products can often distort local expenditure patterns, and create tensions and frustrations — or worse — for millions of people.

The implications of globalisation for women: a gender analysis

In looking at globalisation from a gender perspective, we need not only to find out how, and in what ways, women or men win or lose in the globalisation process, and to trace the (often nefarious) impact of globalisation on women. We also need to map out the different aspects of the globalisation process, and view each of these aspects through the lens of gender analysis. Only if we do this will we gain detailed insights into women and men's livelihood struggles. These insights will enable us to create policies, organisations, and institutions that will further the process of sustainable human development for families, neighbourhoods, and countries in the twenty-first century.

A gender perspective on contemporary globalisation however, must be framed in terms of the historical reality of international economic and social policies in the 1980s and 1990s. This era was dominated by economic policies designed to compel indebted developing countries to restructure their economies and become solvent within the world economy. These policies, collectively known as structural adjustment packages, were the price demanded by the World Bank and the IMF in exchange for extending financial assistance and credit to such countries (Watt 2000). But the packages were based on economic models that were indifferent to gender divisions in household and national economies, and ignored the needs of populations for health and education services as the foundation for human resource development, and the family requirements for unpaid reproductive labour involved in child nurturing, care of the sick, disabled, and elderly, and community management (Elson 1995).

It is perhaps most straightforward to trace the economic implications of globalisation for women in terms of the employment generated by the expansion of global trade and production. As has been long acknowledged, the majority of the workforce in the new sectors producing consumption goods and services for global markets are women — in clothing and sportswear, in electronics components and consumer goods, in data entry facilities and financial services call centres, in fruit orchards and flower farms (UN 1999). Tourism, another by-product of economic internationalisation, also provides a high proportion of jobs for women. However, across these sectors, the evidence is that women are still largely confined to lower-paid occupations. Indeed, a feature of contemporary globalisation is the trend towards the flexibilisation of labour, including part-time, casual, and informal-sector jobs (including home-based work), and women are over-represented in all these sectors (UN 1999). In rural areas, evidence suggests that women still perform the bulk of tasks in subsistence agriculture. Meanwhile, increasing commercialisation of agriculture, as well as landlessness and impoverishment have meant that women as well as men have had to develop a portfolio of income-earning activities, including petty trade, services and artisan production, to meet the increasing cost of household survival. Surviving is a task made all the more difficult by the global trend towards user charges on basic social services, including education and health care.

In many ways, women have become the ideal 'flexible' workers in the new global economy, in the sense that their widespread incorporation into global labour markets has given them little security or bargaining power in relation to wages, working conditions, and entitlements to non-wage benefits and publicly provided repro-ductive services such as child care, elderly care or unemployment benefits or pensions (Pearson forthcoming). Moreover, the global features of the modern world economy have meant that new employment opportunities are vulnerable to externally induced economic crisis. The collapse of the south and east Asian economies a few years ago left many former women factory workers unemployed: reports indicate that 10,000 women workers in South Korea were laid off every day, while those whose earnings wholly or partially supported their families' survival had to face reductions in real wages of up to 100 per cent within a six-month period (Panos 1999). Women workers within the global economy are also vulnerable to the fact that their working conditions are often unregulated and unprotected. For example, there is much evidence that electronics workers suffer a range of hazards to their health, including

their reproductive health, while the health of women working in seasonal export agriculture is harmed by chemical fertilisers and pesticides, and those working on computer terminals can suffer from repetitive strain injury and radiation effects (Pearson 1995).

Women's employment has been a key aspect of recent changes in global production and trade, particularly in labour-intensive manufacturing such as electronics, garments, and sportswear (Pearson 1998), data entry (Pearson and Mitter 1993; Dunn and Dunn 1999) and teleservices (Reardon 1999; Mitter 1999). Yet, there is evidence that ongoing technical change may actually override the reasons why women have become the preferred labour force in many industries. For example, automated fabrication and assembly can replace women's dextrous and accurate labour on electronics assembly lines; the worldwide web could replace call centres; and direct computer entry can replace data entry employment.[4] The fact that the demand for women's employment may decrease in this way in the coming decades highlights the structural problems women face in obtaining access to the technical skills and training required for their full participation in the new knowledge-based economy[5] that is such a key feature of globalisation.

Other aspects of globalisation also interlock with economic need to present problems and vulnerabilities for women. The growth of the international transport, tourism, and entertainment industries has fuelled demand for the trafficking of women for sexual services. Rising numbers of sex workers — legal, semi-legal and illegal — are an acknowledged aspect of the global reach of services and markets, which should not be overlooked in any analysis of globalisation (Pettman 1996).

While globalisation has resulted in women's increasing involvement in production and paid employment, most are

14

retaining their primary responsibility for reproductive activities in an increasing unstable world. The rising participation of women in waged labour destroys any illusion that men have a unique role as family breadwinners, and this requires a difficult adjustment for current and future generations of men. At the same time, there is little evidence that men are significantly taking on more of what has traditionally been women's domestic labour, causing stress and conflict in many households (Koch Laier 1997). In situations where traditional sources of employment and income generation are no longer available, many men — and some women — are forced to migrate to other parts of the country or even to other countries and continents, splitting families and communities. While globalisation is challenging women in terms of increased and changing participation in the paid economy, there is no doubt that men's roles are also being challenged by globalisation processes; these are causing increasing polarisation in terms of access to education, training, and employment, and high levels of migration, separating men from their families and communities. The economic and social trends outlined above leave many women unsupported in their challenge to make a living and bring up their children.

The internationalisation of tastes referred to earlier places women and men living in poverty in the centre of a global consumption nexus, mediating between children whose demands are formulated through international media and imagery, and limited economic resources. A manifestation of the gendered nature of such global tastes lies with the hegemony of football as the world sport *par excellence* — primarily (though not solely) a masculine activity with a multi-billion-dollar spin-off industry of clothing, equipment, media, and communication products. Women and girls too are subject

to the relentless global marketing of fashion clothing and accessories, and 'modern', Western-style furniture and décor. Internationalisation of consumption not only reinforces and expands a gendered demand for consumption spending, which may itself cause inter-gender and intergenerational conflict, particularly in households with limited incomes, but also puts additional strain on women who are most frequently the individuals required to balance the competing demands on household budgets (Engle 1995).

Response or resistance to globalisation: the role of the international women's movement

Women's perspectives and gender issues have been increasingly prominent on the international stage since the First United Nations Conference in Mexico City in 1975 marked the start of the UN Decade for Women 1976–85. However, the debates of the Mexico City meeting were firmly rooted in a pre-global order of national and international politics.

One response to the increasing level of economic globalisation is the attempt to regulate international trade and investment through the activities of transnational bodies such as the World Trade Organisation (WTO). However, as the events surrounding the WTO negotiations in Seattle in December 1999 indicate, the terms on which the global economy is to be regulated are being fought out not just between national governments and representatives of transnational corporations (TNCs) and labour organisations, but also by a large range of organisations from across the spectrum of civil society. In a sense, the response to the Seattle trade talks reflects the multi-dimensional nature of globalisation, and the difficulties of trying to contain its forces within a purely economic and technical sphere.[6]

The quarter of a century since the Mexico City meeting has witnessed an inter-nationalisation of feminist activism, asserting that economic and technical issues must be seen in their social and political context. Over the last years of the 20th century, women's organisations and lobby groups emerged as the transnational political actor *par excellence*. Women's perspectives have not been limited to the quinquennial United Nations meetings on women and development meetings, but have been central to key international conferences on the environment (Rio in 1992), human rights (Vienna, 1993), population (Cairo, 1994) and social develop-ment (Copenhagen, 1995). Globalisation of technology, and of economic regulation and production has afforded opportunities to the international women's movement to insist that women's perspectives are central to international policy and governance. They have resulted in important acknowl-edgements at international fora of the interlinked nature of economic, social, and political change, including the importance of environmental management for sustainable livelihoods; women's human right to freedom from violence in the home and the public sphere; the need for reproductive rights being mainstreamed into population and family planning policy; and the central importance of unpaid work in the family and community for the economic wellbeing of the public economy.

This mainstreaming of gender concerns in international policy fora has resulted in the formulation and reform of laws, ensuring that it is more than mere lip service to politically correct opinion. For example, the recognition that women have the right to freedom from violence and bodily integrity as a basic human right has been translated into the addition of rape as an international war crime, and several war trials following the conflicts in the Balkans and in Rwanda have concretely reflected this change in public policy.

Global feminist action has also resulted in changes of policy on the part of international development bodies. An example here is the current international concern about the exclusion of women and girls from employment, education, and health care in Afghanistan. Both aid agencies and international organisations have reiterated their commitment to the principle of equitable development, and negotiations for development assistance in Afghanistan have centred on issues of equitable access and resources for women and men (Emmott 1999). The broader issue of the rise of fundamentalism all over the world — and the control on women's lives, education, and marriage exercised in the name of adherence to religious texts — is also being challenged on the grounds of universal human rights of women.

International solidarity between women in different parts of the world is being assisted greatly by the new commu-nications technologies associated with globalisation. For instance, there is a new campaign against the practice of female genital mutilation (FGM), supported by Womankind Worldwide, a UK-based NGO. FGM is a practice rationalised in the name of culture and tradition, but which has long been contested by African women in the continent and in the diaspora. The Womankind Worldwide programme is building on this opposition by facilitating the creation of an international coalition of women's groups from a range of African countries and Northern countries. It is using the world wide web to share experiences, knowledge of health and legal practices and devise strategies for advocacy and awareness campaigns).[7]

A further illustration of the current incorporation of gender concerns at a global policy level is the current discussions at the IMF and the World Bank on the proposed Global Standard for Social Policy. Proposals for this draw on the 1995 United Nations Social Summit in Copenhagen and its

Platform for Action. They cover general principles in the following four areas: achieving access to basic social services; enabling all men and women to attain secure and sustainable livelihoods, and decent working conditions; promoting systems of social protection; and fostering social integration[8] (Norton 1999). Although such discussions are at a very early stage, they reflect a recognition of the interconnectedness of production and reproduction, which has been the basis of gender analyses of the global economy over the past 30 years. This recognition itself reflects the growing realisation on the part of economic policy-makers that they cannot continue to limit their policy analysis to the formal employment sector, but instead have a responsibility for the majority of producers in the developing world, who work in self-employed, family-based or informal forms of labour and therefore fall outside formal systems of social protection.

The problems for women arising from their incorporation into the global economy are real and ever-present. But so, too, are initiatives seeking to extend guarantees of the ILO's Core Labour Standards to all international production and global trade. While the internationalisation of global consumption patterns will continue to accentuate the pressure on women responsible for making family budgets viable, international consumer pressure has also been responsible for a range of initiatives including Voluntary Codes of Conduct to safeguard the working conditions of workers involved in the production of a range of consumer products including sportswear, clothing, and fruit and vegetables. While such initiatives cover both men and women some of the most far reaching Codes of Conduct are those drawn up by and for women workers. These cover non-wage benefits, sexual harassment, security and safety of employment, and serve as a model for other workers in global production chains (Seyfang 1999).

The challenges for gender of globalisation

There are many who have reacted against the global incorporation of gender issues into the NGO and development agenda, contending that it reflects a Western imperialist bias and indicates opposition to appropriate local social relations and practices. However, the robustness of the challenge on gender issues from feminist activists and gender and development policy-makers to development policy and institutions in the last third of the twentieth century indicates that its relevance transcends the local. The indications are that the new century will witness an assertion of the global relevance of gender in development not just by gender advocates, but by development institutions and organisations concerned with meeting the challenges of globalisation (Sen 1997); extending the application of gender analysis to men as well as women, and encouraging the creative application of gender-equitable policies to new generations and contexts.

While the constraints and inequalities produced by economic and technological globalisation will provide the backdrop necessary for international and local campaigning, advocacy, and policy design and implementation, they also offer the opportunities for new and appropriate initiatives. I will conclude by mentioning a project recently initiated in a small British provincial town, Norwich. Called 'Moving the Goalposts', it has as its objective the promotion of girls' football in an area around Mombasa in Kenya.[9] It seeks to provide training for local girls, links with girls' and community football projects in Norwich through educational and fund-raising activities, and ultimately through international exchange visits and tournaments. This was an initiative that came in the wake of the Woman's Football World Cup in 1999, which attracted a great deal of international intention, but it was also inspired by an existing girls' football team of some years' standing in Kilifi, eastern Kenya. In seeking to empower young women in both Kenya and the UK, the project demonstrates a fresh and innovative approach to gender and development. It offers the opportunity to capture the interest of an entire new generation in a new context, promote international understanding and learning, and use global communications in a positive way. Such a project is the product of internationalisation — of sport, of media, of communications and product markets — and an example of how women's activism and imagination can be used to subvert the gendered stereotypes of international sport. It may not have the weight of the international sports and leisure industry behind it, but it provides an indication of the fluidity of gender relations in a global world, and the sense that there is everything to play for.

Ruth Pearson is Professor of Development Studies, University of Leeds, Leeds LS2 9JT, UK. E-mail: r.pearson@leeds.ac.uk

Notes

1 The various academic and political positions on globalisation and its implications in different regions are well covered in Lechner, Frank J and Boli, John (eds) (2000) *The Globalization Reader*, Blackwell Publishers, Oxford.

2 The 'third industrial revolution' refers to the great changes in production technology that followed the development of micro-electronics and biotechnology, leading to the production of a range of new products, as well as to their incorporation into existing products such as cars and television sets. The application of micro-electronic and computer technology to telecommunications has further revolutionised a range of production processes, and catalysed the development of new products and services such as mobile telephones and the worldwide web. Most importantly, it has made possible not just international communications, but international control and dispersion of production and services.

3 For further discussion of world cities and globalisation see leGates, RT and Stout, F (eds) (1996) *The City Reader*, Routledge, UK.

4 A call centre is a relatively new and fast-growing kind of production site where service functions are carried out over the telephone, for a range of enterprises including sales, banking and financial services, inland revenue (tax) offices, airline and travel companies. Telephone interaction replaces (or less commonly complements) face-to-face interaction with the customer. Call centres are offices, usually fairly large in scale, and may operate for a single operation or handle teleservices for a range of contractors. See Richardson (1999). Further information can be found on http://www.callcentreworld.com/

5 The knowledge economy refers to the increasing displacement of physical labour (usually men's) and manually dextrous and docile labour (usually women's), required in sectors such as micro-electronic assembly, garments, food production, data-entry, and tele-services) with technically trained and qualified labour, predominantly male. See World Bank 1999.

6 For more discussion on the WTO, see the *Globalization Reader*, op cit (note 1).

7 Website: http//www.womankind.org.uk /cpgfgm.htm. For more information on Womankind Worldwide see Resources section, p 115.

8 Social protection refers to systems (usually run by the state) of social security and income support for the unemployed, the elderly and the sick. Social integration refers to the combating of social exclusion (a term increasingly used to denote not only economic poverty, but exclusion from opportunities in the labour market, education and services).

9 This project is organised by a local women's group who have applied to the UK National Lottery for funding. A current fundraising activity is a so-called 'bootlink' in which local (to Norwich) football-playing girls are encouraged to donate second-hand football boots and other kit to be donated to the much poorer teams in Kenya.

References

Blumberg, RL, Rakowski, CA, Tinker, I and Monteon, M (eds) (1995) *Engendering Wealth and Well-being: Empowerment for global change*, Westview Press.

Dunn, L and Dunn, HS (1999) *Employment, Working Conditions and Labour Relations in Offshore Data Service Enterprises: Case studies of Barbados and Jamaica*, Multinational Enterprises Programme Working paper No 86 ILO, Geneva.

Emmott, S (1999) 'Personnel management in a time of crisis: experience from Afghanistan' in Porter F, Smyth, I and Sweetman, C (eds) (1999) *Gender Works: Oxfam experience in policy and practice*, Oxfam GB, Oxford.

Engle, P (1995) 'Father's Money, Mother's Money, and Parental Commitment: Guatemala and Nicaragua' in Blumberg et al. (eds) (1995).

Elson, D (1995) *Male Bias in the Development Process*, Manchester University Press.

Giddens, A (1999) *Runaway World: How globalisation is re-shaping our lives*, Profile Books, London.

Koch Laier, J (1997) 'Women's Work and the Household in Latin America: A Discussion of the Literature', CDR Working Paper 97, Centre for Development Research, Copenhagen.

Norton, A (1999) 'Can there be a Global Standard for Social Policy? The Social Policy Principles as a Test Case', ODI Briefing Paper (draft), October.

Mitter, S (1999) 'Globalization, Technological Changes and the Search for a New Paradigm for Women's Work', *Gender, Technology and Development*, 3:1.

Mitter, S and Bastos, M-I (eds) (1999), *Europe and Developing Countries in the Globalised Information Economy: Employment and distance education*, Routledge, UK.

Panos (1999) *Globalisation and Employment: New opportunities, real threats* (1999), Panos Briefing No 33 May (Panos briefings can be obtained from PANOS 9 White Lion Street, London, N1 9PD, UK. Tel +44 (0)20 7278 0345; e-mail: panoslondon@gn.apc,org; website: http://www.oneworld.org/panos/

Pearson, R (1995) 'Gender perspectives on health and safety in information processing: Learning from international experience', in Mitter, S and Rowbotham, S (eds) (1995) *Women Encounter Technology: Changing Patterns of Employment in the Third World*, Routledge, UK.

Pearson, R (Dec 2000, forthcoming) 'All Change? Women, men and reproductive work in the global economy', in *European Journal of Development Research*.

Pettman, J (1996) 'An international political economy of sex?', in Kofman, E and Youngs, G (eds) *Globalization: Theory and Practice*, Pinter, London.

Reardon, G (1999) 'Telebanking: Breaking the logic of spatial and work organisation', in Mitter, S and Bastos, M-I (eds) (1999).

Richardson, R (1999) 'Call centres and the prospects for export-oriented work in the developing world', in Mitter, S and Bastos, M-I (eds) (1999).

Sassen, S (1991) *The Global City: New York, London and Tokyo*, Princeton University Press.

Sassen, S (1998) *Globalization and its Discontents*, The New Press.

Sen, G (1997) 'Globalization in the 21st Century: Challenges for civil society', University of Amsterdam Development lecture 1997. Available from the Institute for Development Research Amsterdam (IDRA), University of Amsterdam, Plantage Muidergracht 12, 1018 TV Amsterdam, The Netherlands; e-mail: j.r.muller@frw.uva.nl

Seyfang, G (1999) 'Private Sector Self-Regulation for Social Responsibility: Mapping codes of conduct', Working Paper No 1, Research Project on Ethical Trading and Globalisation, Overseas Development Group, UEA, December.

UN (1999) *1999 Survey on the Role of Women in Development: Globalization, Gender and Work*, UN Division for the Advancement of Women, Department of Economic and Social Affairs, New York.

Watt, P (2000) *Social Investment and Economic Growth: A strategy to eradicate poverty*, Oxfam GB, Oxford.

World Bank (1998) *Knowledge for Development: World Bank Report 1998/9*, Washington DC.

Gender, globalisation, and democracy

Sylvia Walby

Women's presence in democratically elected assemblies around the world has increased, and women have been participating in the wave of democratisation during the 1990s. While the proportion of parliamentary seats held by women is not in itself a sufficient indicator of women's representation in politics, it is an important factor in reflections on gender equity and development.

Globalisation has often been represented as a process which is hostile to democracy, yet globalisation and democratisation have been taking place at the same time. Despite the rise of global financial markets and corporations — which are widely believed to reduce the political capacity of nation-states (Held 1995) — there has been not only a third wave of democratisation (Huntington 1991) and immediate suffrage for women in the new democracies, but also an increase of women in existing parliaments (Inter-Parliamentary Union [IPU] 1995).

While it can be important to grasp the detail of the particularity of women's lives, we must not lose sight of the larger picture of global and regional linkages and changes, especially in an era of globalisation. Much contemporary feminist scholarship has argued for a focus on the particular, on the specific, rather than the large scale of global; it has focused on difference and diversity rather than commonality. This argument is often positioned as a rejection of essentialism and of a false universalism based on the experiences of dominant white Western women. However, while the attention to diversity has been an important dimension of feminist analysis, it has led to a relative neglect of the larger scale of social change, especially globalisation. Feminist analysis needs to address global change, and the global future needs to be gendered.

The political dimensions of globalisation

While much attention has been focused on the economic dimensions of globalisation, some of the political dimensions are as important. Globalising processes may be undermining the capacity of nation-states to act autonomously, but some aspects of these processes are facilitating the development of certain democratic procedures.

Globalisation is not a uniform process with a single direction, and one can identify many paradoxes: increased numbers of highly educated skilled workers, even though global capital appears to seek cheap labour; more democratic governments alongside the greater power of multinational companies and financial markets; increased calls for the state's protection of human rights at the same time as its role in providing welfare is eroding; and increases in the spread of education and literacy, simultaneous with the growing power of global financial markets (Walby 2001).

Analysis of globalisation has sometimes been polarised between those who think that globalisation produces uniformity or homogenisation (Fukuyama 1992; Ohmae 1995) and those who think that particularity or heterogeneity is maintained by different cultural responses to ostensibly similar global pressures (Robertson 1992). Rather than catalysing convergence or divergence in social relations, globalisation catalyses transformation.

But how is globalisation gendered? What are the changes in women's participation in formal parliamentary politics on a global scale? To what extent are these related to a country's internal economic and political situation rather than external pressures? What are the implications of increased global flows at a political level for achieving women's democratic political expression and power? Is there a connection between economic development and political democracy for women?

This article uses recent data from the Inter-Parliamentary Union (1995, 1999a, 1999b), the UNDP (1995, 1997, 1999), and the ILO (1996). Since these data are relatively easily accessible, the raw data will not be reproduced here. This global level of analysis is intended as an addition, rather than an alternative, to case-study analysis.

Gender and development approaches and democracy

The analysis of gender relations within processes of development planning has been authoritatively described by Moser (1993) in her influential distinction between five approaches: welfare; three Women in Development approaches: equity, anti-poverty, and efficiency; and empowerment. The earliest approach, welfare, was seen merely as trying to develop women as better

mothers. The second approach sought to gain equity for women, but was seen as based on Western concepts rather than endogenous feminism. The anti-poverty approach focused on poor women in order to improve their productivity, but tended to isolate poor women as a separate category. The efficiency approach focused on improving the efficiency of the local economy by drawing on the contributions of women, but was problematic in its tendency merely to extend women's working time. The fifth approach, empowerment, was seen as seeking to empower women through greater self-reliance, and to have a 'bottom-up' rather than 'top-down' orientation, but because of its focus on women's self-reliance tended to be unsupported by governments, leading to slow growth of under-financed voluntary organisations.

A new approach

A sixth approach which combines efficiency and empowerment needs to be added, one which sees democratisation and efficiency going hand-in-hand, and for women as well as for men. This would highlight the problematic nature of the direction of causality assumed in the traditional 'modernisation' theory of development, by suggesting not that liberal democracy is the outcome of economic modernisation, but that economic modernisation requires a free and democratic society (Leftwich 1996). Such an approach is facilitated by the end of the cold war, and, indeed, some see the fall of communism as proof of such an approach (Huntington 1991), because it is associated with the increased interest in the role of a 'free' civil society in underpinning a democratic state (Cohen and Arato 1995; Potter et al. 1997). The new approach is based on the understanding that a modern economy needs people to be educated and to be able to associate freely and to exchange information; further, that democracy is an efficient way to control the vested interests which might otherwise dominate and corrupt the state, harming its potential for ensuring development (Castells 1996).

It is unnecessary to set up a false dichotomy between the efficiency and empowerment approaches to gender-sensitive development interventions. Rather, they are interdependent, and should be synthesised in the sixth approach described above. This approach, captured in the shorthand 'productive engagement', has the potential to become well-known and of widespread use.

While most work within this emergent perspective pays little attention to gender, it is incomplete without a gender dimension. There can be no democracy if women are not full political participants. Not only must women's empowerment be a focus for grassroots organisations (as was typical in the early empowerment approach), it must also be a focus for the state and the institutions of global governance. In order for an economy and a society to be productive, women as well as men need to be engaged fully, which can only effectively happen if the state, as well civil society, is democratic.

In the rest of this article, I shall examine the evidence which has emerged in support of a 'productive engagement' approach, examining the rise of women's participation in parliaments around the world, and its association both with economic and human development and with regional and global political alliances.

The rise in women's representation in national parliaments

Since 1945, there has been a major increase in the extent to which women are elected as representatives in national parliaments around the world (Table 1). This started from a very low base indeed, and everywhere, women's representation in parliaments is still lower than men's. Nevertheless, there have been major changes.

During the course of the twentieth century, women have won the right to vote in most countries of the world, with three major waves in 1918-20, 1945-46, and during decolonisation. But the right to vote did not immediately mean that women were elected to parliaments; this has been a very slow development.

This increase in women in parliaments has overlapped with a general 'third wave' of democratisation (Huntington 1991), although the rise in women's representation is of longer duration. A higher proportion of countries have democratically elected assemblies today than 20 years ago. This in itself increases the number of women in parliaments. The third wave has involved important changes for women as well as for men, although this is barely noted in otherwise wide-ranging texts on democratisation (Huntington 1991; Potter et al. 1997).

Table 1: Percentage of women MPs in national parliaments around the world

Year	1945	1955	1965	1975	1985	1995	1999
Percentage of women MPs	3.0	7.5	8.1	10.9	12.0	11.6	13.2
Number of parliaments	26	61	94	115	136	176	179

NB These include all national assemblies, whether or not they meet conventional definitions of membership through democratic elections.
Source: IPU 1997, 1999a, 1999b.

Variations

The pattern of women' representation in parliaments is very variable between different countries; a few of the reasons will be mentioned here.

There is a regional pattern, although there are significant variations within each region. The Nordic countries have the highest representation of women, with female parliament membership at 38.9 per cent, while that of Europe is 15.5 per cent, Asia 14.9 per cent, the Americas 14.7 per cent, sub-Saharan Africa 10.9 per cent, the Pacific region 8.7 per cent, and Arab states 3.8 per cent (IPU 1999a).

Some types of electoral system are associated with higher proportions of women elected. In particular, these include multi-member constituencies, where electors get to choose several candidates from a list, and proportional representation rather than the first-past-the-post system, so second-choice candidates get a chance to be elected. Countries with these electoral systems tend to have higher proportions of women MPs than those who do not, probably by removing the pressure to vote for just one candidate who is more likely to be a man, and replacing this with incentives to get a 'balanced' set of representatives (Lovenduski and Norris 1993; IPU 1997).

Unsurprisingly, countries in which women have had suffrage for longer tend to have higher proportions of elected women in parliament.

Non-democratic parliaments and women's representation

Not everyone agrees that there has been a steady increase in women's parliamentary representation. Petersen and Runyan (1999) suggest that the proportion has 'stagnated'. They report that the peak of women's parliamentary representation was reached in 1988 when women made up 14.8 per cent of elected members of parliament world-wide. However, this pessimistic conclusion depends on an equation of parliamentary with democratic representation.

To be fair to Petersen and Runyan, they do not say that all the parliaments they consider are democratic. They use IPU data, which includes all parliaments, whether or not the membership is through democratic elections. In particular, the IPU data includes the parliaments of Eastern Europe during the communist period. It is very unusual to consider these parliaments as democratic, because of the limitations on the number of parties allowed to contest elections and on free debate. During the period from 1945 to 1989, women constituted about one-third of the membership of these assemblies in Eastern Europe and the Soviet Union. The transition to a market economy and more open democracy was accompanied by a dramatic drop in the number of women in the national assemblies. Very recently, this has been growing again. It appears, therefore, that it is the dramatic changes in Eastern Europe which account for the apparent stagnation and fall in women's presence in national assemblies between 1988 (14.8 per cent) and 1994 (11 per cent). However, if these assemblies are removed from the world averages, then the proportion of women in national parliaments shows a continuing upward trajectory, with no stagnation or fall.

Explaining the increase in women elected to national parliaments

There are two main factors behind the rise in women's election to parliaments: the increase of women's economic power; and women's political struggles.

Women's employment

There is a correlation between the proportion of women in employment and parliament in many countries. The countries which have the highest proportion of women elected to the national parliament have high rates of paid employment among women. For instance, the Nordic countries have the highest rates of female membership of parliaments in the world, and among the highest rates of female employment. Sweden (42.7 per cent of MPs), Denmark (37.4 per cent of MPs), Finland (37.0 per cent of MPs) and Norway (36.4 per cent of MPs) have more women in parliament than anywhere else (IPU 1999b), and women's employment as a percentage of men's is high in Sweden (90 per cent), Denmark (84.7 per cent), Finland (87.3 per cent) and Norway (83.8 per cent), compared with a world average of 69.8 per cent (UNDP 1999, 233). In comparison, countries with low levels of representation of women in parliament also have low rates of female paid employment. For instance, among the Arab states, women make up 3.8 per cent of members of parliament, and women's employment as a percentage of men's is 38.6 per cent — the lowest on both indicators for any region of the world (UNDP 1999).

More interesting for those considering what will occur in the twenty-first century is the change in political representation and employment levels over time. In many countries, the proportion of women in parliament has grown significantly in the same period during which women's paid employment has grown. Thirty years ago, the Nordic countries had quite modest levels of women in parliament, at a time when their female employment was comparatively low. The pattern of strong parliamentary representation and high levels of female employment is not an unchanging essential feature of Nordic societies, but a phenomenon of the last quarter of the twentieth century. For instance, in Norway in 1970, women's economic activity rate[1] was only 40 per cent of that of men — considerably less than the 1977 average for the developing world of 68 per cent. In 1970, 9 per cent of MPs in Norway were female, similar to the rate of 10 per cent among developing countries in 1999 (UNDP 1995,

1999; IPU 1995). This means that an increase of women's employment, under particular circumstances, can make an increase in women's parliamentary representation likely. Table 2 provides examples of countries where there has been an increase both in women's employment and their parliamentary representation between 1970 and 1995. (Data for all countries can be found in the UNDP annual reports, by combining tables. The table is selective rather than representative.)

The correlation between the increase in women's parliamentary representation and women's proportion of paid employment is stronger in industrialised countries than in non-industrialised countries. This is partly because the category 'paid employment' better fits contexts where work outside the household is likely to be paid and that within the household unpaid; it has a less certain meaning in societies with a large agricultural sector, where the boundaries between paid and unpaid work, and between the public and domestic sphere, are less likely to coincide .

Of course, industrialisation does not necessarily lead to an increase in women's employment, as Boserup (1970) noted long ago. Indeed, Pampel and Tanaka (1986) show that the relationship between industrialisation and women's employment is described by a U-shaped curve: women's employment declines in the early stages of industrialisation and rises later on. Thus it is important not to conflate industrialisation with women's waged employment, but to keep them separate in any analysis (Walby 1990), which traditional modernisation theory did not. The focus here is specifically on the correlation between a rise in women's employment and a rise in their representation in parliament.

The failure of traditional modernisation theory (Lipset 1960) to make the distinction between industrialisation and the increase in women's paid employment is one of the reasons why it does not recognise the link

Table 2: Women's economic activity rates as a percentage of men's in 1970 and 1994; female percentage of parliamentary seats in 1970 and 1995

Country	Women's economic activity as a percentage of men's		Female percentage of parliament (lower or single house)	
	1970	1994	1970	1995
Canada	47	63	0.4	18
USA	53	65	2	11
Jamaica	67	82	4	12
Barbados	54	78	0	11
Honduras	17	27	3	7
Guatemala	15	21	2	8
Guyana	25	34	12	20
Finland	70	82	17	34
Norway	40	68	9	39
Sweden	54	77	14	40
Denmark	54	77	11	34
France	53	64	2	6
Spain	22	31	1	16
UK	51	60	4	9
Ireland	35	41	2	12
United Arab Emirates	9	23	0	0
Tunisia	13	33	4	7
Egypt	7	12	1	2
South Africa	47	54		25
Zambia	34	41	2	7
Sri Lanka	37	36	4	5
Australia	45	61	0	9

Sources: derived from UNDP (1995) Annex Table A2.3; IPU (1995) 'Women in Parliaments 1945-1995: A World Statistical Survey Series', Reports and Documents no. 23, Geneva.

between economic development and women's access to political democracy. In order to understand the nature of the connection between modernisation and changes in gender relations, it is necessary to undertake a gender analysis of both the nature of the economic changes and the nature of the political changes.

Women's political struggles

Women's political struggles have been a significant factor in gaining the vote and representation for women in most places. However, the rise in women's parliamentary representation is linked, not only to specific national struggles, but to regional and global political alliances. Democratisation is a political movement which is not confined to nation-states, but one which draws strength from regional and global political linkages. Four illustrations of this are given here: the first female suffrage wave, when women demanded the vote; decolonisation and suffrage (voting rights for all new citizens); the role of women's voices in the regulation of male violence; and women and development.

The first female suffrage movement was international, based in several northern European countries and North American countries. The vote might have been a tool within nation-state politics, but women's suffrage was advanced by an internationally connected movement. The timing of the vote for women around the North Atlantic rim in about 1918 cannot be attributed to a particular level of economic development, since the timing both of industrialisation and of women's entry into employment was very varied, ranging from the mid-eighteenth to mid-twentieth century. For instance, while women in the UK and Sweden won the suffrage at nearly the same time — 1918 and 1928 in the UK, 1919 in Sweden — both industrialisation and women's entry into waged work took place a lot earlier in the UK than in Sweden. This means that in Sweden political citizenship was won for women before industrialisation, while, in the UK, entry to the waged labour market preceded entry to parliament. The suffrage movement crossed national boundaries because of the links between activists in countries in the same region of the world.

Decolonisation was a global political movement, although it involved specific foci on the dominant colonial powers. In the vast majority of countries freed from colonial rule during the twentieth century, suffrage was granted to men and women at the same time. Even where feminism was seen as a Western invention, women's suffrage was seen as a human right (Jayawardena 1986; Ramirez, et al. 1997).

There are many examples of feminist global alliances since the 1970s. These have successfully utilised institutions of emerging global governance such as the UN and the World Bank, as spaces within which feminist politics can be built. An example of this has been the campaign to put the regulation of men's violence against women on the global political agenda, and thereby on the domestic agenda of specific nation-states. A feminist advocacy network (Keck and Sikkink 1998) successfully established that women's rights should be equated with human rights, and that this included the right not to be beaten or raped. An international feminist campaign won agreement at the 1993 United Nations World Conference on Human Rights in Vienna that women's rights were human rights (Peters and Wolper 1995). This established a context in which it could be successfully argued that violence against women constituted a violation of women's human rights, as was achieved in the Declaration and Platform for Action at the 1995 UN Conference in Beijing. This movement was decentralised, and not led from any one country, yet it created a powerful international feminist alliance. It was successful in building a campaign that draws on the notion of universal human rights, while at the same time respecting the cultural differences between women, holding in creative tension both 'universalism' and sensitivity to particular contexts. While not succeeding in instigating a strong legal response to violence against women, nevertheless, the issue has been placed on national agendas through the concerted efforts both of feminist activists around the world and of women members of national parliaments.

The Women in Development movement is a further example of a global feminist advocacy network (Waylen 1996; Moser 1993) which engages with both international bodies and national parliaments. This is crucial in a context where states are still significant political actors, despite globalisation.

While women's struggles are varied in their specific goals and organisational formats, and uneven in the extent of their mobilisation, they share the goal of improving women's position in society. They are also variously successful in their struggles. While the lack of success may be attributed to organisational failure, it is sometimes better explained by the hostility of the particular context (Walby 1997). Thus, in addition to asking whether and how women organise to achieve particular goals, we must inquire about the particular conditions under which they struggle. This focus on the context of women's political struggles returns us to the significance of their economic context.

Conclusion

Feminists have often been sceptical of the claims of modernisation theory, because of its overly simplistic assertions that development will be good for women (Boserup 1970; Waylen 1996; Petersen and Runyan 1999). Yet sometimes this pessimism can go too far. Often, globalisation has been seen in terms of its capacity to undermine democratic forms of politics (Held 1995) and criticised accordingly; yet feminist politics is an example of globalisation *assisting* democratic politics in certain contexts. This assistance is patchy, of course, and, indeed, unequal access to new global forms of communication such as the internet is likely to result in unequal access to political decision-making. But globalisation does produce new opportunities for feminist politics as well as new difficulties.

First, there is the emergent position of 'productive engagement', in which an efficient economy and a democratic society are seen as interdependent. There is a steady increase in the proportion of women in parliaments around the world; women are increasing their participation in paid employment; and some women, in some places, are gaining some kinds of empowerment. While there are many caveats — that the work is badly paid; that the proportion of women in parliament is too low — nonetheless these developments provide a basis on which some women can enhance their capacities and capabilities.

The increase in parliamentary representation does correlate to some extent with an increase in women's paid employment, especially in the more industrialised countries. This gives an indication that women are able to transfer power from one arena to another, under certain circumstances; but the connection is far from complete. One of the reasons for the relative lack of fit between increase in parliamentary representation and paid employment is that feminist politics are less constrained by the borders of nation-states than are women's opportunities for employment. Women's suffrage politics in particular have always been regional at the very least, and are now global. Women in one place derive support from others elsewhere; international feminist linkages have made a difference.

While it will always be important to consider the differences between cultures and between women, we should not omit to consider both commonalities and the scope for alliances between women from diverse contexts. Globalisation is a gendered process which is restructuring social relations on a large scale. As well as challenges, it presents opportunities for women in development.

Sylvia Walby is Professor of Sociology, Department of Sociology & Social Policy, University of Leeds, Leeds LS2 9JT, UK. E-mail: s.walby@leeds.ac.uk

Note

1 Economic activity refers to people in paid employment as well as to those seeking it.

References

Boserup, E (1970) *Women's Role in Economic Development*, Allen & Unwin, London.

Castells, M (1996) *The Information Age: Economy, Society and Culture; Volume 1: The Rise of the Network Society*, Blackwell, Oxford.

Cohen, J and Arato A (1992) *Civil Society and Political Theory*, MIT Press, Cambridge, Massachusetts.

Fukuyama, F (1992) *The End of History and the Last Man*, Penguin, London.

Held, D (1995) *Democracy and the Global Order: From modern state to cosmopolitan governance*, Polity Press, Cambridge.

Huntington, SP (1991) *The Third Wave: Democratization in the late twentieth century*, University of Oklahoma Press.

Inter-Parliamentary Union (1995) *Women in Parliaments: 1945-1995: A World Statistical Survey*, IPU, Geneva.

Inter-Parliamentary Union (1997) *Men and Women in Politics: Democracy still in the making; A World Comparative Survey*, IPU, Geneva.

Inter-Parliamentary Union (1999a) 'Women in National Parliaments: World average; regional averages',
http://www.ipu.org/wmn-e/world.htm

Inter-Parliamentary Union (1999b) Women in National Parliaments: World classification',
http://www.ipu.org/wmn-e/classif.htm

Kandiyoti, D (ed) (1991) *Women, Islam and the State*, Macmillan, Basingstoke.

Keck, M and Sikkink, K (1998) *Activists Beyond Borders: Advocacy networks in international politics*, Cornell University Press, Ithaca, New York.

Leftwich, A (ed) (1996) *Democracy and Development*, Polity Press, Cambridge.

Lipset, SM (1960) *Political Man: The social bases of politics*, Heinemann, London.

Lovenduski, J and Norris P (ed) (1993) *Gender and Party Politics*, Sage, London.

Martin, H-P and Schumann, H (1997) *The Global Trap: Globalization and the assault on democracy and prosperity*, Zed Press, London.

Moser, Caroline (1993) *Gender Planning and Development: Theory, practice and training*, Routledge, London.

Ohmae, K (1995) *The End of the Nation State: The Rise of Regional Economics*, Harper Collins, London.

Pampel, FC and Kazuko T (1986) 'Economic Development and female labour force participation: A reconsideration', *Social Forces*, 64:3, 599-619.

Petersen, VS and Runyan AS (1999) *Global Gender Issues*, Westview Press, Boulder, Colorado.

Peters, J and Wolper, A (eds) (1995) *Women's Rights: Human Rights: International feminist perspectives*, Routledge, London.

Potter, D, Goldblatt D, Kiloh M and Lewis P (eds) (1997) *Democratization*, Polity Press, Cambridge.

Ramirez, FO, Soysal Y, Shanahan S (1997) 'The changing logic of political citizenship: cross-national acquisition of women's suffrage rights, 1890-1990', *American Sociological Review*, 1997, 62, 735-745.

Robertson, R (1992) *Globalization: Social theory and global culture*, Sage, London.

UNDP (1995) *Human Development Report*, Oxford University Press, New York.

UNDP (1999) *Human Development Report*, Oxford University Press, New York.

Walby, S (1990) *Theorizing Patriarchy*, Blackwell, Oxford.

Walby, S (1997) *Gender Transformations*, Routledge, London.

Walby, S (2001 forthcoming) *Modernity and Globalisation*, Sage, London.

Waylen, G (1996) *Gender in Third World Politics*, Open University Press, Buckingham.

Globalisation and gender training for the media:

Challenges and lessons learned

Patricia A. Made

The 1995 Beijing Conference on Women identified the media as one of the critical areas of concern for the advancement of women's equality and development. In an era of globalisation, its role in the struggle for gender equality is critical. This article discusses the author's experience of developing gender training for media professionals.

The media have the power to shape attitudes, to perpetuate the status quo, or to instigate change. Media professionals' lack of knowledge of gender and development is one of the major challenges facing not only the international women's movement, but also media professionals like myself who are involved in training our colleagues.

Three years ago, during a gender training programme for journalists in Harare, Zimbabwe, the group was asked to define the word 'gender', one of the common terms used in the discourse on women's rights and development. Anonymously, each journalist wrote a definition of the term on a card, which were then pasted to the wall for everyone to see. All kinds of definitions of gender were given: 'women's fight for equality'; 'women attacking men'; 'women fighting for their rights'; and many others.

When the correct definition of gender — those differences between men and women which are socially constructed, can change over time, and vary within and between cultures — was announced, many of the journalists were stunned. One brave male journalist even questioned the correct definition. He argued that his definition of gender, as women fighting for their rights, had to be the correct one — because this was what he had read in the media (personal experience, 1997). If even those who work in the media are 'victims' of the wrong information and messages that are printed or broadcast daily, one can imagine the impact on millions of viewers, listeners, and readers worldwide.

The media are a key institutional player in holding governments and other institutions accountable for adhering to the democratic ideals of transparency, accountability and 'good governance', which must include equality for women and men. To date, the media have positively influenced public attitudes on many issues of human rights, but failed to challenge gender-based discrimination in societies across the world. The 1995 Beijing Platform for Action stated that 'the lack of gender sensitivity in the media is evidenced by the failure to eliminate the gender-based stereotyping that can be found in the public and private, local, national and international media organisations' (Beijing Platform for Action, Section J, 133).

In addition to their role in promoting positive images of women and educating the public on gender equality, the media also have a social responsibility to self-regulate in order to avoid indecent, degrading, or exploitative depictions of women. At present, the Beijing Platform for Action points out that '...the print and electronic media in most countries do not provide a balanced picture of women's diverse lives and contributions to society in a changing world. In addition, violent and degrading or pornographic media products are also negatively affecting women and their participation in society. Programming that reinforces women's traditional roles can be equally limiting' (ibid., 133).

The current process of globalisation has implications for the regulation of the media: as electronic methods of communications proliferate, state regulation will become increasingly difficult. Margaret Gallagher, a media consultant, has observed that 'with the globalisation of markets, economic affairs are becoming more and more detached from social concerns. As multi-media conglomerates increasingly gain control of world information and communication markets, public authorities are less and less able to impose or maintain controls — to the detriment of the most vulnerable groups in society. With media regulation becoming more and more difficult to enforce, and with the media increasingly driven by the quest for huge financial profit, the commodification of women in media content is likely to intensify'.

The IPS experience

This article discusses the experience of Inter Press Service (IPS), a global information and communications service which is set up as a not-for-profit association of journalists, in re-training media professionals to challenge their views on gender issues. We have introduced new training programmes, tools, and curricula to enable the media to report more analytically and competently on gender issues. This is groundbreaking work with the potential to transform the media and to ensure that gender stereotypes are broken, and women's views and priorities represented.

Since its founding in 1964, IPS has become a major information provider, which seeks to promote the principles of human rights, democracy, and good governance through its system of inter-cultural communications. Integral to IPS's principles is the dissemination of information that heightens awareness of the inequality between women and men, and of information which can be used as a key tool in advocacy and lobbying efforts by civil society in eliminating gender inequality and discrimination. It aims to develop a global communications strategy, bringing together the media, civil society, and policy-makers, at national, regional, and international levels.

The agency now covers news and issues in Africa, the Asia-Pacific region, Latin America, North America, Europe, and the Caribbean, through a network of full-time correspondents and freelance journalists. The agency has regional offices and editorial headquarters in Africa, the Asia-Pacific region, Latin America, North America, and Europe, and a World Editing Desk in Mexico. IPS has grown rapidly, which has prompted a constant review of its founding principles and a commitment to 'introspective change'. We have realised, like many other organisations, that we need to face the challenge of bridging the gap between our commitment and good intentions, and putting these into practice; so over the past four years, we have worked to strengthen the gender perspective in our news coverage.

IPS's work on gender

First, the agency examined gender roles and responsibilities within the organisation and reviewed its organisational structure.

Women now hold key posts as regional directors, as project officers who develop programmes and policies; the interim head of IPS is a woman. We have learned through practical experience that training and re-training journalists to report fairly on gender is not only about teaching new concepts, but more importantly, it is about changing the way journalists go about gathering information, and setting the 'news agenda'.

The second step, which coincided with the first, was creating gender-responsive editorial and employment policies to guide the agency's work towards better practices. IPS Africa was the first regional centre to develop the first policy. Gender analysis is not only a key tool in effecting change in the voices and perspectives presented in our editorial coverage of news, but also in ensuring positive change for women in our own organisation.

After developing the policy, the next step was training. At the outset, the training took the format of seminars, and what the agency refers to as 'on-line' training: editors provide guidance for the writing and development of stories through messages sent to journalists using e-mail and the internet. When stories are sent into the editing centres, editors read them for style, content, sourcing, background information, and data, and often send back queries to correspondents and stringers[1] when information is missing. This method, used within the agency for a number of years, has helped to improve the quality of writing received from freelance and young journalists learning how to write for the media.

As the agency progressed through the process of policy development, we began to see the challenges of gender 'mainstreaming': that is, integrating the concepts of gender, equality, and women's rights into all our editorial coverage, and ensuring that these issues influence our news agenda. IPS carried out a range of activities in the various regions of the network between 1994 and 1999 to develop guidelines, provide training, and develop gender tools that could be used by the journalists on their desks to improve further their reporting of gender issues. One of these tools was a glossary of terms common in gender and development discourse. This glossary has been produced in English and Spanish, and the agency is now working on French and Portuguese editions.

Challenges of gender training for the media

Developing any training programme for the media in a new area presents an array of challenges; one needs to find creative ways to ensure that media professionals grasp that the issue is 'news', to be consistently covered. Below are several of the challenges that IPS has experienced in training on gender issues.

Understanding the basics

The first challenge is to ensure that journalists and editors understand the issues and the concepts, in order to report them competently and accurately. We cannot assume that when we refer to terms including 'gender', 'equity', 'equality', and 'empowerment of women' that journalists and editors automatically understand what these terms mean.

People have formed definitions of these terms based on their experiences and through discussions with others, which may often be misleading or wrong. This then translates into the communication of wrong or negative messages when the terms are used in articles or broadcasts about women and their development in relation to men in a society. So the first challenge is to treat gender and development like a specialised area of reporting, thereby crafting training programmes which start with the basics of defining the terms.

Dispelling the myth of 'hard' and 'soft' news

A major challenge is the false distinction between 'hard' and 'soft' news in journalism, which has marginalised women in the major issues which determine men's and women's relationships and the course of development. 'Hard' news, which focuses on gender-blind analyses of current events, politics, and macroeconomics, is seen as the guts of journalism. 'Soft' news includes reporting on social sectors, including health, education, and 'women's issues', which are isolated on separate pages, or in programmes or magazines which are aimed entirely at women. The topics covered in 'women's pages' tend not to be analytical, even though they may include practical issues, for example cookery and children's health, in line with the stereotype of women as primary carers for families.

However, the distinction between 'hard' and 'soft' news is false, as is the association of 'soft' news with women's concerns. It has become clear that gender-based discrimination is a cross-cutting issue which affects political and economic, as well as social, development. We can no longer, for example, talk about economic development without talking about the issue of poverty, and the data show that the majority of the world's poor are women. Using a gender analysis to examine 'hard news' stories enables us to find hidden stories which are of interest and relevance to all readers.

Moving from awareness-raising to providing professional tools

Another challenge is to present journalists with professional tools which they can use every day, rather than rely only on awareness-raising. Over the past 15 years, gender training for various professional groups has become quite an industry. While some journalists have undergone gender training, this has not a discernible impact on the content of programmes and print media. To be effective in moving beyond awareness-raising, those involved in training must craft a well-designed training programme that puts the principles of gender equality into practice, by showing journalists what needs to be done differently in their daily job of deciding on a 'news agenda' and gathering and disseminating newsworthy information.

This is a big challenge. How do we craft journalistic training or re-training programmes that provide the media with gender analysis tools which can be used in their day-to-day work? For example, such a tool might provide them with a set of new questions which must be asked when they are doing a story, to assess the impact of an event on women and men. Another might show them how to redefine their idea of news, in order to ensure the incorporation of a gender analysis. We may attempt to provide such tools, for example by raising the question of gender-sensitive language, and of the way in which women and men are portrayed; but how often do we revisit the interviewing techniques which are fundamental to gathering information? Is information gathered from men and women in the same way? What new techniques might need to be incorporated to ensure that increasingly, journalists go to women as sources of information as a matter of course, leading to more of their voices and perspectives in printed stories and broadcasts? What new data must be used in writing or compiling stories for print media or broadcast, and how do journalists source it?

IPS's response

When we trained the journalists within the IPS network, the gender training was designed specifically to meet the staff's needs and priority issues. For example, training in Africa focused on gender and human rights, while the Caribbean region decided to introduce gender and development concepts. However, it is clear that we need a much more holistic and comprehensive training approach, in addition to developing curricula on how to incorporate gender even further into specialised areas of journalism, including environment, technology, and economics.

Developing training manuals helps to take the message beyond the few who sit in a seminar or short course. Crucial, too, is the fact that the development of the manuals and tools begin to ground gender as a journalistic discipline. Manuals need to be on hand in news rooms, in training institutions, and with non-government and other groups wishing to work with the media. These manuals should include gender glossaries which not only define terms, but also give examples of usage.

We also need training tools on specialised areas. At IPS, we are currently developing a training manual entitled 'How to report on gender violence'. This has been a two-year endeavour: we tested aspects of the manual in two small sessions in Southern Africa, and plan to test it further and produce it in 2000 for use by the media and non-government organisations working with the media.

Lessons we have learned

Policy is the first step to mainstreaming

Policy guides the process of change. Developing an editorial and employment policy on gender is key, and a major step in the process of changing the media's treatment of women. Once a policy is developed, especially a gender-responsive editorial policy, it becomes a tool for guiding the editors' and journalists' work, and things are not left to the biases that men and women editors and journalists have grown accustomed to over a long period of time.

In IPS, every region developed a policy on gender, which were subsequently taken up and 'owned' at senior level. We then identified ways to implement the policies within the framework of the news agency's

work. Once a policy has been developed, implementation needs to occur through it being constantly promoted by the editors, who are key to determining what issues are covered and who set the news agenda.

We think that our policy is proving successful for several reasons:

- It ensured commitment within the agency at the highest levels of management (central and regional).

- Through seminars, the policy was developed with the participation of senior editors and correspondents, rather than externally or by top management. Therefore, those who had ultimate responsibility for implementing and guiding the policy, both men and women, took ownership of it.

- Having a policy helped to overcome resistance from correspondents and stringers who were not used to going to women for information, or who saw women as not having credible opinions on political and economic issues outside culture and social issues.

Training is the key to change

Training enhances skills, and provides the opportunity to reflect on and question continually how we cover issues. In particular, professional training of the kind suggested earlier will take journalists from being 'gender-aware' to being 'gender-responsive' in their coverage of all issues. However, we have learned that training will only remain effective if it is built upon by subsequent programmes which reinforce earlier gender training. It cannot be a one-off activity.

It is far easier to preach than to practise

Mainstreaming gender into the news coverage, or strengthening the gender perspective in news, is a process which takes time, commitment, and effort. The process must be worked on in a concerted and consistent way.

Keep track of the progress

We must devise tools for evaluating progress, so that the weaknesses of our work can be addressed. So far, an annual analysis of IPS's editorial content is done by the Communications School at the University of Washington in Seattle, USA. However, it focuses in the main on quantitative data (the extent to which women have been used as sources for news). We need to devise tools for qualitative analysis.

The importance of new partnerships

In the regions where IPS works, its experience of trying to mainstream gender into its work has precipitated the forging of new partnerships with organisations working on women's rights and gender and development. These organisations have become key sources of information to IPS journalists, and have also been partners in developing seminars and training programmes for correspondents and editors.

This partnership also has provided IPS with new audiences: information targeted at the media has been re-packaged into electronic mail bulletins, specifically for non-government groups and policy-makers. We compile a free weekly news bulletin on gender and human rights, which is disseminated worldwide via e-mail. (Readers interested should send an e-mail to tafadzwa@ipsafrica.org; lamine@ipsafrica.org; or pat@ipsafrica.org.)

Finally, IPS is joining forces with UNIFEM in the first six months of 2000, to send its e-mail bulletin subscribers a series of 15 profiles portraying the lives of women leaders at community, regional, national, and international level. The central focus of the series is to capture, through their own voices and of those around them, the diverse leadership styles and the achievements of women who are contributing to sustainable development and change in their societies. As the world prepares for the 'Beijing +5' Review at the United Nations in June 2000, this special IPS series meets one of the specific action points in the 1995 Beijing Platform for Action: 'to produce and/or disseminate media materials on women leaders, inter alia, as leaders who bring to their positions of leadership many different experiences'. The features will appear at the end of every month, and will be drawn from Africa, the Asia-Pacific region, Latin America, North America, and the Caribbean.

Patricia A. Made is Interim Director of Inter Press Service News Agency, PO Box 6050, Harare, Zimbabwe. E-mail: pat@ips.org

Note

1 People who provide the media with information on news in particular contexts.

Reference

Gallagher M (undated), 'Some Issues in the Gender and Media Debate', in *Women, Media and Violence*, a WACC Women's Programme publication.

Women's labour and economic globalisation:
A participatory workshop created by Alternative Women in Development (Alt-WID)

Carol Barton and Elmira Nazombei[1]

Alt-WID, a working group of feminist educators and activists formed in 1993, focuses on the relationships between global macroeconomic policies and conditions in our local communities. The group is particularly interested in translating ideas into popular education tools that can be used by organisers and grassroots groups. This article describes one of their workshops.

Alt-WID aims to bridge the gaps in analyses of human rights and economic justice in both North and South from a feminist perspective (which integrates awareness of gender, race, and class differentiation). Alt-WID has particularly focused on promoting women's right to work, to social protection, bodily integrity, and an adequate standard of living, concepts which have emerged from the UN Universal Declaration of Human Rights of 1948 and the 1966 UN Covenant on Economic and Social Rights. Human rights lawyers and women's organisations tend to neglect economic and social rights, while development organisations which are concerned with these issues have tended to be weak on gender analysis. (The name we chose for our group shows our awareness of the way in which many international development organisations have merely tried to add a gender perspective to the dominant development agenda.)

Our aim in developing public education tools through participatory work is to draw from participants' knowledge and experience, and enable them to build a collective analysis of a situation, ultimately leading to action. This article describes Alt-WID's Women's Labour and Economic Globalisation Workshop, which we have presented in various contexts in the USA, primarily with women activists working at the local, national, or international level. Most recently, we ran the workshop at the Association for Women in Development (AWID) conference, held in Washington in November 1999. Rather than confining ourselves to a report on the outcomes of the AWID workshop, we are writing this article as a guide for other trainers, outlining the aims and method of the workshop as well as providing the materials. Finally, we summarise the kinds of topics participants have raised so far.

Aims of the workshop

The purpose of the workshop is to consider the varied roles that women play in the global economy, and to consider their experiences in the light of those rights which they are entitled to as member of families, communities, nations, and the international community. The workshop features a series of anecdotes to illustrate the diverse ways in which globalisation affects women in all regions of the world. Our working assumption is that women's labour is the lynch-pin of globalisation: the global economy would not be able to function without women's paid and unpaid labour — from work in sweatshops and factories, to work in forced prostitution, to increasing unpaid work for the community. Very often, however, women's labour, paid or unpaid, is undervalued in both monetary and social terms.

To do this, we ask participants to consider fictional, composite accounts which have been created from real women's experiences. We choose different accounts depending on the group, because we consider it essential to have at least one anecdote which relates closely to the group's own experience, and one which represents a very different reality.

Questions are posed to encourage participants to consider the connections between different women's experiences of globalisation, and the institutions and value systems that shape their contexts. The workshop aims to enable participants to look beyond local and national circumstances, to the 'layers of causality' which shape their specific experience of globalisation. Participants analyse different scenarios to explore which human rights are violated, which individual and institutional actors are causing the violation, which policies are at work, and which underlying values support these policies. Participants specifically examine which impacts are gender-specific, and which disproportionately affect women. They go on to consider why this is the case. We then take time to discuss the individual, community-based, and institutional actions necessary to bring about change.

The workshop schedule

We estimate a minimum running time for this workshop of three hours, with the following elements.

Introduction (15 minutes)

Here, we use a brief exercise to make the group members feel comfortable, to learn more about them and about their own experiences in relation to the theme of economic globalisation[2].

Plenary: Identifying Women's Human Rights (15 minutes)

We use a wall-sized sticky cloth in order to construct a version of the grid seen in the handouts detailed below, with the four 'rights' categories on the left, and headings ranged across the top. As the group names specific rights, we write them on coloured paper and begin to sort them into the categories (work, bodily integrity, social protection, and adequate standard of living). We then have a brief discussion about what human rights laws ('instruments') exist, how economic human rights are identified, and why we think it is useful to explore globalisation within a rights framework. We hand out copies of the Universal Declaration of Human Rights and the Economic and Social Covenant for reference.

Small group work: The vignettes (45 minutes)

We divide the group into four small groups (or multiples of four if it is large) and give each one an anecdote to work on (see below). Each group is also given a hand-out with these questions:

- What human rights are implicated in this situation?
- What are the policies at work that specifically or disproportionately affect women's rights in this situation?
- Which institutions, organisations, governments and/or value systems are responsible?

Participants are asked to read and discuss the anecdote, and discuss the questions. We also hand out four grids (see opposite) which they can use if they wish. The goal is to begin from the lived experience of a woman, and to identify the policies, actors, and values that shape her situation.

Handout 1: Women's labour and economic globalisation: Identifying women's rights

Rights	Rights identified
Work	
Personal safety	
Basic services	
Adequate standard of living (access to land, jobs, education, credit, and so on)	

Handout 2: Women's labour and economic globalisation: Rights, experience, policies/practices

Rights	Policies/practices: gender-specific	Policies/practices: disproportionate impact
Work		
Personal safety		
Basic services		
Adequate standard of living (access to land, jobs, education, credit, and so on)		

Handout 3: Women's labour and economic globalisation: Actors

Rights	Persons	Institutions	Governments	Value systems
Work				
Personal safety				
Basic services				
Adequate standard of living (access to land, jobs, education, credit, and so on)				

Handout 4: Women's labour and economic globalisation: Current strategies for action

Rights	Personal	Communal	Institutional
Work			
Personal safety			
Basic services			
Adequate standard of living (access to land, jobs, education, credit, and so on)			

Plenary: Building a group analysis (1 hour)

The small groups come back together, and each group briefly tells the others the story of the woman whose account they discussed. They share their insights about causality. As they report back, we build an overarching analysis by putting up their observations on the wall-sized grid. We may interrupt from time to time in order to ask questions or to encourage discussion on a specific point. For example, if a group identifies that a woman has had her right to an adequate standard of living violated, and the policy that has resulted in this is 'welfare reform' in the USA, we may encourage a discussion of the specific dynamics which led to that policy — who wins and who loses? In this discussion, we might ask participants to think about which consequences of this policy disproportionately affect women (such as layoffs in a female-dominated industry), and which are based on stereotypes of gender relations in society (such as policies against hiring women of child-bearing age). This aims to deepen our understanding of the gendered nature of globalisation.

Plenary: Discussion of alternatives to the existing policies (30 mins)

As a group, we collectively discuss the values inherent in the policies discussed, and consider alternatives. We try to steer towards examples of current, concrete alternatives to the policies discussed, because we have found that otherwise it can get very abstract (such as 'end patriarchy'), which is demotivating. We suggest that if you have time, and the workshop participants plan to work together beyond the workshop itself, this is the moment to discuss what this particular group might do together.

Individually and in plenary: Evaluation (15 minutes)

The workshop always ends with participants giving written feedback, as well as communicating it in a group discussion which focuses on the process of the workshop and the group's discoveries.

The anecdotes

Here are four very different accounts of the kind used at our workshops:

A Filipina 'entertainment' worker in Japan

Fely is 18 years old and works as a 'dancer' in Tokyo. She comes from a very poor rural community in the Philippines. Two years ago, she left her village because her family could not earn enough money to support her brothers and sisters. Her parents hoped that she might find a job in Manila, and be able to send money home to the family.

Fely lived in Manila with her cousin, but for two months was unable to find work. She was about to give up when her cousin told her that she had heard that the government's Overseas Employment Administration had a special service to help women who want to work overseas. She learned that in order to earn hard currency to help pay its foreign debts, the government had been advised by the World Bank to encourage its citizens to work abroad, where the demand for cheap labour is great. The government agency said that jobs for women were especially plentiful. Some estimate the remittances from Filipino overseas workers at as much as US$2 million a year. Fely remembered that her cousin Lea had left the Philippines several years ago to work in Japan, and the whole family relies on the money she sends home.

Fely's cousin helped her find a 'broker', who told her that he could arrange for her to have a job as a 'dancer'. He promised to arrange for a passport and to pay her airfare. He promised that she would have no trouble paying him back with the large salary she would be earning in Japan.

When Fely arrived in Japan she discovered that her broker had sold her to another man for US$8,000. This man owned a bar/brothel, and her job would not be dancing, but prostitution. Fely felt frightened and desperate, but she had no choice but to go along with the bar owner's plans. In the weeks that followed, she learned that the bar where she worked, and many others, are controlled by crime syndicates, and that the sex industry in Japan is worth trillions of yen. The success of Japanese companies at home and abroad has earned some people high incomes, and excess wealth has increased demands for the sex industry. Fely knows that some of the money goes to bribe corrupt passport officials and other bureaucrats. She has noticed that when police officers come to the bar they receive free services from the bar girls. The other girls in the bar tell her that they have heard that there may be as many as 150,000 Filipina women working as prostitutes in Japan.

Fely has never found her cousin Lea, but now she hopes that she is not somewhere else in Toyko leading a life similar to her own. Fely wishes that she could return to Manila but she knows that she will have to work for a long time to pay back the bar owner. She knows that her family is making good use of the money that she is able to send back home. Sometimes she wonders why people think so little of women that they must face such a difficult life. She knows that she has never met a Filipino man in Japan who has been forced to endure the abuse that she faces daily.

A 'workfare' worker in New York

Helen is an African American woman living in New York City. She is 35 years old and mother of two young children. She receives public assistance[3], but is facing a cut-off in her benefits, because the city authorities have created a 'workfare' programme, under which all recipients of public assistance have to work, mostly cleaning the parks and subways. More than 37,000 people are now working for their benefits in New York City. More than 17,000 workfare recipients have signed a petition requesting the right to form a union, but the city argues that they are not workers, so they cannot form a union. At the same time, 20,000 unionised public sector workers have lost their jobs. Workfare recipients now form one-third of the Sanitation Department's workforce. They earn below the statutory minimum wage, and are still below the poverty line. They are supposedly acquiring transferable skills, so that they can go on to a permanent job, but street-cleaning gives them no skills, and it is often dangerous. One elderly woman died of a heart attack when she was forced to work despite making complaints. Workfare recipients are denied coats and protective gloves, and are exposed to hazardous materials. Helen and her friends consider it slave labour. From what Helen sees, the workfare programme in New York is mostly made up of Latina and African American women, and now the Mayor is insisting that disabled mothers also take part in the scheme. The city administration is also threatening to deny subsidised housing to women who don't work outside the home.

Helen used to go to the City College, and was able to use her public assistance money to pay for child-care. However, now she must pay for child-care during the hours she spends on workfare, and has had to give up her education. Also, the classes conflict with her work schedule. Moreover, the city authorities are cutting back on classes and tightening admissions, so fewer poor students and immigrant students can attend. Helen is also seeing cuts in her children's school's budget, as class sizes get bigger and there are fewer materials. The schools her children attend can't afford the computers and resources that other schools catering for richer children have.

Helen has heard that if every new job created in New York were given to a welfare recipient, it would take 21 years for all of them to get a job! Even in a boom economy, it is clear that there are not enough jobs to go round — much less good jobs with benefits. Some of her friends have got off public assistance by taking poorly paid jobs or temporary jobs, but they don't last. Low-paid jobs don't offer health insurance, and it's hard to cover child-care costs. Helen is scared of what will happen to her and her children.

African rural woman

Wanjiku is 30, and lives on a small farm with her mother-in-law in the Central Province of Kenya, less than 100 miles from Nairobi. She has three children, two in primary school and one at home. Wanjiku went to school up to the age of 12. Although she passed the exam to go on to secondary school, her parents did not have money to send her. She worked at home on the farm with her mother, taking care of her younger brothers and sisters until she was 17, when she got married. Her husband has a job as a messenger in Nairobi, and comes home about once a month.

Before Wanjiku left her mother's farm, one of her responsibilities was selling in the market. Wanjiku would take the maize and other vegetables that her mother grew and sit in the market and sell them. Her mother used the money she earned to pay school fees and buy school uniforms for Wanjiku's younger brothers and sisters.

Wanjiku had hoped to grow vegetables herself to sell, in order to send her own children to primary school. But during his last visit, her husband told her that the government had been told by some international experts that there is much more money to be made in growing flowers for export to Germany. The experts said that the only way Kenya could get loans to help with its debt repayments and to strengthen its economy would be to grow more cash crops. Wanjiku's husband thinks that the government will give him a loan to help him start growing flowers, and told her that she must forget about vegetables. When Wanjiku asked him what the children were going to eat, since those vegetables were also their food, he laughed and said that they would be able to buy all the food they needed with the money they could make from flowers. She knows that until the profits from the flowers come in, she will need to use the remaining food carefully and make sure that her two sons that are in school eat their fill first.

Today, Wanjiku's young daughter is sick with diarrhoea. Wanjiku has decided not to walk to the health clinic in the village to see the nurse because she does not have the fee that the clinic now charges, and she hopes that she can treat her at home with some herbal remedies.

A maquiladora worker in Mexico

Reynalda works in a maquila plant in Monterrey, Mexico, assembling electronic products for export to the US. She is 20 years old and has worked at the factory for four years. She discovered this year that she has carpal tunnel syndrome[4], and may not be able to continue to work. A US company owns her factory, but companies from Japan, Korea, and Germany also employ women workers in Monterrey. Almost all of the workers in her plant are women; they work long hours for minimal pay. There are no unions, and if they try to form one, they know they will lose their jobs. Reynalda and her friends dress up smartly to go to work because the bosses like it. Sometimes they are sexually harassed, but they are frightened of losing their jobs if they don't acquiesce. The bosses prefer to employ young, unmarried women who are unlikely to challenge them, and who will obey orders.

It's hard for some Reynalda's married friends to keep working at the factory, because of child-care and the extra demands on them: but they do it because they need the money. There are other problems for mothers: in one border town, they know of babies who were born without a spine, which is attributed to pollution from the plant. In Reynalda's plant they are told to wear masks, but these don't seem to protect them from the toxic fumes. The mask instructions are written in

English, so she is not exactly sure of what they say. The pollution is also affecting the community's water and land near the factories. Everyone is concerned about what is happening. They want to complain and to change things, but work is scarce, and lots of others are waiting in line for jobs.

Many women have come to the city from the countryside, as large-scale agricultural enterprises run by large corporations are moving in and displacing small farmers, following the repeal of laws that safeguarded their land titles. Reynalda has heard that this new legislation is part of the policies Mexico had to adopt because of its huge foreign debt. In order to get new loans, the IMF and World Bank want to see changes. Mexico sold state companies to private firms, and invited in foreign companies. Mexico is now exporting vegetables, but importing corn, its staple crop. At the same time, the government cut food subsidies, so prices for basic goods keep going up, and more people in the family have to work. It's easier for the women to get these jobs, so Reynalda hangs on at the factory.

Workshop outcomes

Discussing what rights the women in the anecdotes need to have recognised, workshop participants identified the right to economic independence and to work. At work, they have the right to safe and healthy working conditions and a living wage, to equal pay for equal work, and the right to organise in unions. They have a right for their children to be cared for while they are working, or to look after their own children. They have a right to reasonable working hours and paid holidays. They have a right to control over their own bodies, to health-care and housing. Finally, they have the right to live in their own country, and to freedom of movement.

In discussing gender-specific violations of rights, workshop participants at AWID mentioned ways in which gender stereotypes of women's work shape their experience of it under globalisation:

'A lot of women's work is unpaid and unremunerated.'

'Some women are held in servitude for economic and sexual exploitation.'

'Many women are denied the right to control their own money.'

'Men are often still regarded as the primary income-earner, leading to lower pay for women.'
'Pensions go to the "head of family".'

'Women in employment face discrimination due to pregnancy and child-care.'

'The image of a worker is male-biased.'

'Lower female literacy rates mean lower-paying jobs.'

'Women in higher-paying professions face both formal and informal occupational segregation.'

'Women's work and women's status is not adequately measured, so there is little acknowledgement of their contribution and protection.'

'Women are often the last hired, first fired.'

'The traditional care-giving skills women have are not valued.'

'In some contexts, women are not allowed to work outside the home, in others they are forced to do so.'

The group summarised this by pointing out that international economic policies are based on fundamentally discriminatory assumptions about the nature and conditions of women's work.

Identifying the causes

The small groups at the AWID workshop also explored how economic changes brought about by globalisation affect gender relations between men and women. Their points included:

- sexual harassment (women's economic conditions may make it harder for them to challenge this);

- the growth of the informal sector of the economy, in which women predominate;

- women migrant workers — for example for sex work or domestic work — have no legal status or rights to protect them against exploitation and abuse;

- women agricultural workers — those working for their families — may earn nothing. Those employed in agribusiness may have few safeguards on their rights and may earn very little;

- competition for jobs forces workers to take unsafe and poorly paid work, or to migrate;

- some laws which are supposed to protect are used to discriminate;

- the growth of contracted labour and home work, particularly in sectors such as textiles, has relied on women workers;

- cuts in the public sector and social services, including education, health-care, and child-care, have resulted in increased unpaid labour for women;

- families often prioritise boys' education;

- in industrialised countries, cuts in public assistance have forced women to leave their children to work at sub-minimum wages;

- the migration of women weakens family support systems and increases violence against children;

- the increase in male migration leaves women to care for families on their own.

Looking at macroeconomic policies and relevant actors and institutions, AWID participants focused on the process of corporate restructuring that has led to 'downsizing' operations in industrialised countries, sub-contracting to smaller companies and individual home-workers (which undermines principles of wages and conditions and prevents workers from organising in unions), and the growth of sweatshops and maquilas in 'developing' countries. These trends have relied on women as a flexible workforce in need of paid employment. Participants also discussed the role of the IMF and World Bank in prescribing structural adjustment policies (SAPs) in the 1980s and 1990s, which have promoted privatisation, deregulation, cuts in social spending, and an opening of markets to foreign direct investment and trade, as well as a reorientation of economies towards export production. They identified the World Trade Organisation (WTO) and trade liberalisation as having a major role in shaping the job market, the health of national economies and national budgets, and ultimately the process of democratic decision-making within states.

Strategies for action

The part of the workshop which is most likely to vary is the final part, when participants are called on to identify possible strategies for action. Some strategies can be taken on by all — for example, popular education and campaigning, including efforts to influence the media. Others are specific to the participants at a particular workshop: for example, a workshop where all participants are women from one industrialised country might decide to support women whose access to public funds is threatened. At a workshop like AWID, where participants come from all over the world and many different institutions, it is possible to address a global problem, such as the trafficking of women. Other global strategies could include local efforts to support civil society organising at the regional and international levels, or to challenge international financial institutions and other global bodies, culminating in mobilisation such as that seen in Seattle for the WTO Ministerial Conference in 1999.

44

Conclusion

As we emphasise at the start of each workshop, women's human rights are not abstract dreams; nor are they merely a set of legal covenants and conventions. Alt-WID has now run this workshop in many fora. These include the Fifty Years is Enough/Jubilee 2000 Conference, the Women's International League for Peace and Freedom Conference, and events run by the Women's International Global Leadership Institute of the Centre for Women's Global Leadership. Clear analyses and inspired strategies for action have originated from women's experience of daily life, their awareness of their dignity as human beings, and the requirement that this human dignity is recognised and enforced through law. Please let us know if you use the workshop; we would welcome a dialogue with any readers who use our methodology, and would also like to have contributions for new accounts of women's lives. Eventually, we hope to publish a collection of anecdotes, which can be used for a range of educational purposes.

Contact details: Alt-WID/NY, c/o MADRE, 121 West 27th Street, #301, New York, NY 10001, USA. Tel: +1 (0)212 627 0444; e-mail: cbarton@igc.org; elmira@rci.rutgers.edu; website: http://www.geocities.com/altwid_ny/ (under construction)

Notes

1 Our thanks to Elena Arengo, Susana Fried, Cathy Powell, Radhika Balakrishnan and all of our Alt-WID/NY colleagues for their role in developing this workshop.
2 Use any suitable ice-breaking exercise. Williams, S et al. (eds) (1994) *The Oxfam Gender Training Manual*, Oxfam GB, Oxford, is a useful source.
3 Economic support from state funds.
4 A disorder also known as repetitive stress injury (RSI), resulting from injury to the median nerve passing from the arm to the hand.

'We are forgotten on earth':
International development targets, poverty, and gender in Ethiopia

Fra von Massow[1]

A team of researchers talked to people living in poverty in Ethiopia to ascertain what stops them from gaining access to affordable, good quality basic health-care services, reproductive health-care services, and primary education. The research findings shed new light on the linkages between limited access to basic services and poverty, low incomes, insecure livelihoods, and poor nutrition.

In 2000, chronic hunger, illiteracy, disease, and the mental anguish which accompanies absolute poverty and unfulfilled aspirations remain a reality for millions of women and men. In mid-1999, a headline in a British daily newspaper announced that the 'UN seeks $50m aid as Ethiopians approach millennium "facing a biblical famine"' (*The Guardian*, 16 July 1999). For me, as for others, the word 'biblical' conjures up ideas of unchanging historical inevitability. However, there is nothing inevitable or historical about modern-day hunger in Ethiopia.

Western nations have pledged to achieve the following international development targets to end absolute poverty by the year 2015.

- To halve the proportion of people living in extreme poverty;

- to achieve universal primary education in all countries[2];

- to demonstrate progress toward gender equality and the empowerment of women by eliminating gender disparity in primary and secondary education by 2005;

- to reduce mortality rates by two-thirds in for infants and children under the age of 5, and reduce rates by three-fourths in maternal mortality;

- to ensure access through the primary health-care system to reproductive health services for all individuals of appropriate ages as soon as possible;

- to ensure that current trends in the loss of environmental resources are effectively reversed at both global and national levels.

(DfID 1997, 21)

Are international resources being made available and allocated in such a way as to ensure that these targets are achieved? This article looks at evidence from Ethiopia, from research carried out from January to March 1999. The research was commissioned by Oxfam GB, as part of a wider health and education research and advocacy project, taking place in Uganda, Mozambique, Vietnam, Philippines, Nicaragua, India, and Ethiopia. Four sites were visited in Ethiopia: Cherkos in Addis Ababa, Delanta in North Wollo, Metta in Eastern Hararge, and Jijiga in Somali Region. The research was led by a team of nine women and men, including the author[3]. About 500 women, men, girls, and boys participated in the research, and 50 people were involved in co-ordinating and implementing the research. Participatory research tools were used in single-sex focus-group discussions, including youth (aged 10-18) and adults. Thirty-five household interviews were conducted at each site, in which women made up 70 per cent of respondents. Government, private, and traditional health-care and education service providers were also interviewed. Thus, local experience, perceptions, and beliefs were compared and linked with those of service providers. Direct quotations in this article are all from people involved in the research (Micro Research Health and Education Ethiopia Site Reports 1-4, and Summary Report, 1999).

Our hypothesis was that, despite the broad consensus that the provision of basic health-care and education services on a gender equitable basis can directly improve human development indicators, access to these services is being eroded in many countries due to deepening poverty and fiscal crises. We focused on access to basic health care, reproductive health care, and primary education. The research aimed to reflect gender and age differences, and to provide disaggregated information. We used the term 'gender' to refer to the social, economic, and political relations between women and men, in which women are often subordinate and disadvantaged. We paid attention to men's roles and experiences of poverty as well as women's, and focused on kinship and households. We recognised that roles of women and men are not natural but socially constructed, capable of change, and context-specific.

As this article shows, the research yielded much evidence to indicate that, with current conditionalities on aid and at current levels of resource allocation, including Western aid, human development targets are unlikely to be reached by the year 2015. Bilateral donors such as the British government's Department for International Development (DfID) are aware of this: 'the resources which the international community has made available to support the development process have declined over recent years' (DfID 1997, 79). At the same time, the number of families suffering absolute poverty in countries including Ethiopia is on the increase.

The findings

Environment, poverty, and food insecurity

In the case of Ethiopia, the population had reached 58.2m by 1997, and is projected to grow to 90.9m by 2015 (UNDP 1999). The World Bank estimates that in Ethiopia there are 19m rural resource poor households, which cannot maintain adequate food security (World Bank 1996, 3).

Climatic changes in countries like Ethiopia are destroying basic subsistence livelihoods in both urban and rural areas. Seven consecutive years of droughts and flooding in northern Ethiopia have affected food security and incomes. Christian Aid estimates that 'the G7 are running up carbon debts[4] in economic efficiency terms of around $13 trillion per year. On the same calculation, the group of highly indebted poor countries (HIPCs) are running up credits of between $141 and $612 billion because of their under-use of fossil fuel resources and the climate.' On this basis they argue that 'industrialised countries should commit significant new resources and technology to help poor countries affected by the increasingly volatile global environment' (Christian Aid 1999, 1). Our research team could see no signs of such investments in identifying and promoting alternative sources of income for poor farmers in Ethiopia. Women in Delanta, North Wollo, said, 'we are forgotten on earth'.

In Ethiopia, as elsewhere in sub-Saharan Africa, livestock represents an important safety net for bad times, and animals are only sold to pay for essential health care and to buy food in 'hungry seasons'. In Jijiga, women explained: 'we measure our wealth by number of cattle. Before, there were differences in the life of people. But these days, all of us go down. All our cattle are dying'. There, the drought had left cattle dead and dying around the village, producing a stench of decay and swarms of flies. Land ownership used to be a sign of wealth, but 'since we can't plough the land without oxen, it serves no purpose.' Persistent poverty and lack of resources affect water resource management and sanitation in all locations. Drought in Jijiga and Delanta exacerbates an already bad situation. Women in Jijiga said: 'when there is rain the stagnant water gets washed away and we can get clear water, but now there is no rain'. In both sites, villagers shared the water hole with livestock and wild animals.

The research findings in all sites confirmed that rural households spend 90-96 per cent of their meagre incomes on food, and still do not have adequate diets. Participants in all rural sites explained how harvests and livestock have been lost as a result of droughts and flooding, and 'all households have become poorer'. As a direct result of lost harvests, a 'levelling off' in poverty was reported in all sites, and 70-80 per cent of households were categorised by participants as 'worst off' (ibid.). The reduction in the number of better off households has a ripple on effect on income sources for poorer households. In Delanta and Jijiga, participants reported that normal share-cropping and livestock-tending arrangements were hardly functioning. In Metta, men from worst-off households no longer had the opportunity to work on wealthier farms because of the drought.

However, households headed by women and those with many small children were said to be least able to cope. Widows, and families with a very sick family member, are considered particularly vulnerable, as are families with little land or no livestock. Having a large family is recognised as a contributor to poverty, as is dependence on erratic and low incomes from daily hired-labour or trading activities. At all sites visited, participants described how dependence on women's low income from labour-intensive trading has increased as a result of the crisis in agriculture. Women said: 'we just use one pot of water for three days because we have nothing to cook. We used to make *injera*[5] and *tella*[6] [also to sell].' Loss of crops also means a loss of women's income from food processing.

This vulnerability affects health, nutrition, and school attendance. A mother in Delanta said: 'my son dropped out of school when he got hungry – a problem for most people here'. At all sites, participants were well acquainted with the signs of malnutrition. About 60 per cent of the poorest households reported eating two meals a day, but a 'meal' at the time of the research often consisted of a handful of roasted grains. In Delanta, over 70 per cent of households reported earnings of less than $6.40 per month for households of five or more persons. Over 90 per cent of income is spent on food. Women and children reported working harder to earn money from collecting and selling firewood and cow dung. The men said that 'we are all struggling selling wood, dung and wool. We are now tired, and the eucalyptus is also lost.' They are aware that they are denuding their own environment in order to survive.

Health care and education: shifts to the 'unpaid economy'

Women in Cherkos, Addis Ababa, told us that 'poverty is a disease in itself.' The negative impact of World Bank and IMF structural adjustment policies on health care and education has been catalogued (Elson 1992). Our findings showed that none of the four sites in Ethiopia had sufficient health-care and education facilities to service the demand for school places, basic health care, and reproductive health care at current population levels. Existing health-care and education facilities are under-resourced: there is a shortage of qualified staff, inadequate supplies of the most commonly needed drugs, and a shortage of water and electricity in hospitals and clinics. Reports of a lack of vehicles and funds for outreach services came from each site, despite the fact that women reported using outreach services until they stopped coming. There is nothing left from household budgets to pay for clothing and exercise books for school, or to treat the most common diseases such as diarrhoea and scabies. In Delanta, one scabies treatment costs $0.35, or two days' work for a woman collecting and selling cow dung as fuel. Malnutrition and water-related diseases affect both sexes and all ages, as does the inability to access health care. Participants told us: 'we just lie on the bed and wait to die'.

In schools, textbooks are shared between four to eight children, and some subjects have no textbooks at all. Average class sizes range from 80 to more than 100, with a sharp fall in attendance after grade 1. Local education authorities and primary schools reported that a high percentage of children were not in school as a result of income poverty, hunger, and child labour, especially girls who contribute to domestic labour. Women's role in earning income becomes ever more important, often using their children's labour. Girls from all sites said that they helped their mothers. In Delanta, girls who collect firewood to sell in the market 15km away pointed out, 'if our fathers could get a harvest we could go to school full time'. Boys in Delanta affirmed: 'We want to stay alive and learn'. However, teachers reported that, should all children of primary school age come to school, there would not be enough places to accommodate them.

As a result of structural adjustment policies, health-care and education services that used to be provided by the 'paid economy' have shifted to the 'unpaid economy' (Elson 1992). In particular, women 'spend more time and energy providing care to the sick, the old and the children amidst increased deaths and malnutrition aggravated by people's low purchasing power and inadequate drugs, medicine and food' (Mukangara and Koda 1997, 21). The Ethiopia research found that the absence of affordable, nearby clinics limits women's choice to home-based or traditional treatments and birth attendants. This failure to provide primary education and basic health care has had an enormous cost in lives and mental health already, and will result in a low productive and economic capacity of the next generation. In Belhare, Jijiga, where 98 per cent of women and girls and 79 per cent of men and boys in the poorest households are illiterate, the women said: 'if our children were educated we would not be like this.'

Gender equality and women's empowerment

It is widely accepted that women make up a large proportion of the very poorest people. UNIFEM's website states: 'Women are still the poorest of the world's poor, representing 70 percent of the 1.3 billion people who live in absolute poverty. When nearly 900 million women have incomes of less than $1 a day, the association between gender inequality and poverty remains a harrowing reality' (http://www.undp.org/unifem/economic.htm).

The research in Ethiopia is witness to the fact that everyone — men, women, girls, and boys — suffers the physical and psychological trauma of extreme poverty. However, women and girls are without doubt even more disadvantaged, as men and health-care providers confirmed. This is due to their low social status compared with men, their under-representation and low participation in decision-making at all levels, their reproductive health experience (including female genital mutilation, early marriage, and multiple pregnancies), and labour-intensive domestic and productive work. In Addis Ababa and Delanta, women from the poorest households believe that women and girls 'can last longer without food', so they have a smaller share. Traditional healers reported treating women for severe abdominal pains attributed to carrying heavy loads over long distances.

Men were aware of, and expressed concern about, women's low nutrition, enormous reproductive health burden, and heavy workload. However, they appeared powerless to shift the traditional gender division of labour. Although men and boys from the poorest households reportedly sometimes help to collect water for the household, they never perform other domestic tasks. It is women's and girls' designated role to maintain the household on a daily basis. In Cherkos, Addis Ababa, men said that women are responsible for all domestic work according to tradition and religion. Outside the household, women continue to be represented by men in the traditional governing structures of the community, which organise and manage community affairs in the absence of active local government structures.

In order that 'they don't suffer like us', as one mother in Addis Ababa put it, women would like their girls to attend school. Others, for example in Jijiga, did not see the point of sending girls to school, 'when all they are going to do is build homes and grind grain'. Youth groups and schools said that parents' low appreciation of the value of education, particularly for girls, contributed to low overall attendance rates. While primary school attendance rates are staggeringly low for both girls and boys (65-88 per cent of children in the four sites are not in school), even fewer girls than boys in each site attend school. With heavy workloads and low-income livelihoods, women cannot manage without

their daughters. For those who do enrol, attendance rates are poor. Boys in Delanta reported that 'we miss one to two days of school a week in order to work, and girls miss two to three days to help their mothers who are overburdened'.

Access to reproductive health care for all

Few rural Ethiopian women have access to family health-care programmes unless an outreach clinic services their village. At two sites, infants had not been immunised, and there was no access to ante-natal services, since an international donor had stopped funding the outreach service. In all sites, a shortage of funds for outreach services, mother-and-child health care (MCH), and health education was reported. There are no reproductive health-care services in or near the villages visited. All the women interviewed in the rural sites had delivered their last born in their village, without any trained medical help. Even in Addis Ababa, 52 per cent of women interviewed had also delivered at home. Maternal mortality rates in Ethiopia are amongst the highest in the world at 1,400 per 100,000 live births in 1990, compared to a UK figure of 9 per 100,000 (UNDP 1999).

In all sites except Addis Ababa, early marriage involving girls aged between 12 and 18 is common. It is estimated that 85 per cent of girls and women in Ethiopia are circumcised (Spadacini and Nichols 1998). In the eastern regions of Metta, Eastern Hararge, and Jijiga, Somali Region, the most intrusive form of female genital mutilation (FGM), infibulation[7], is practised during primary school years. 'There is not one girl who is not circumcised,' the women in Metta stated. In Jijiga the girls said that 'stitching is a problem at marriage and delivery.' A doctor in Eastern Hararge confirmed that very few women have trained medical attendants present during delivery, despite the fact that because of FGM, 'problems during delivery are common. Since the outlet is too narrow, this causes obstructed labour'.

The National Committee on Traditional Practices in Ethiopia is running an awareness-raising campaign to eliminate FGM, but the campaign has not yet made an impact in more remote places. In Metta, girls said: 'we don't know what circumcision is for, but our parents are circumcised so they do that for their children.' Another girl commented: 'we have been educated that it is not good to circumcise girls but it still continues to be practised.' The low priority of, and few resources granted to, this work, women's poverty of representation, and the lack of opportunities for self-expression (especially for exploring intimate issues) all slow down the process of change.

Many reproductive health conditions are intricately tied to traditions and a culture of reticence. Teachers explained why girls do not perform as well as boys in school by saying that girls are socialised to be shy and retiring, carry out domestic work, and are not allowed to move as freely as boys. Women may not see reproductive health conditions as health problems. Men in Jijiga perceived women's gynaecological problems as 'Allah's will for women'. They said: 'women do not talk about such problems. They are shy. Even if they are sick they do not tell men about their diseases'. We also found that change is held up because of men's effective exclusion from reproductive health education. Despite men's evident awareness of the problems created by high population density on exhausted land, family health programmes do not target men.

HIV/AIDS (Ethiopia's highest reported incidence is in Addis Ababa) and sexually transmitted diseases (STDs) in particular were often more associated with men's reproductive health. Participants reported that few men go to government health centres for help if they suspect that they are HIV-positive or have a STD, because these health centres require them to name their partners. Participants said that such men prefer the anonymity of drug stores, holy waters, or herbalists.

In Cherkos, Addis Ababa, poverty and youth unemployment have found expression in a considerable increase in male youth delinquency, and alcohol, tobacco, and drug abuse. Girls in Cherkos are afraid of being accosted, abused, and even raped on their way to school. Girls explained that boys suffered from 'mental unrest and disturbance' because of poverty, unemployment, and lack of prospects. Interestingly, it was men (in Addis Ababa) who included early pregnancy and illegal abortions in their list of major health problems, often resulting in life-threatening situations. Abortion is illegal in Ethiopia. In all sites, boys in particular recommended more reproductive health education for their own generation and for their parents.

Discussions from the research

Three areas of concern arising from the research are highlighted here in a brief discussion.

When does poverty become an emergency?

Where is the dividing line between the condition of chronic poverty, affecting the life expectancy of increasing numbers of people, and an emergency situation? Overall, aid to Ethiopia has shifted from relief aid to development aid. During the 1974–91 regime of Mengistu Haile Mariam, 'Western aid for Ethiopia was ... largely restricted, for political reasons, to emergency, or "humanitarian" help' (Pankhurst 1998, 275). This relief aid was channelled through NGOs, but since 1991 there has been an increase in grant aid channelled through the government. A structural adjustment programme first introduced in 1992 led to an increase in the country's debt stock between 1992–94. The World Bank provided loans for the health-care and education sector programmes (Christian Aid 1999, 6-10). Christian Aid estimates that 'as donors did not replace decreasing emergency disbursements with disbursements for development, total aid disbursements decreased' (ibid., 8).

Oxfam's research in Ethiopia demonstrates the need to integrate skills and experience and to run parallel relief and development programmes. For example, men in Jijiga said that they were too weak to plough: 'we need food first'; yet there was no food aid. Oxfam Ethiopia staff were aware that the lack of emergency food aid undermined progress in their development programmes. One of the most common health problems identified by participants in Metta was 'swollen body' (kwashiorkor) among infants. In all sites, teachers said that the children were hungry in school. Yet neither infants nor primary school pupils have access to supplementary feeding. Hunger is as much a cause of low school attendance as the lack of buildings, teachers, and textbooks.

One woman in Metta explained: 'many children get sick and die because of food shortage. For instance, the doctors advise us to give them many kinds of food like eggs and milk. We are obliged to give them once or twice, but we can't give them after that. So most of the children get sick until they can't even walk.' A man in Delanta reported that men were distraught by their inability to produce food: 'We could not afford clothes for the children. We could not provide food and safe water. Due to the drought our wives are malnourished and give birth to unhealthy children.' In all sites, traditional birth attendants attributed anaemia during pregnancy, miscarriages, and excessive bleeding after delivery due to poor nutrition.

Moreover, emergency relief programmes usually focus on water supply and sanitation. 'Why do you think the flies come and land on us? It's because we are dirty', a woman complained in Delanta. In Jijiga, women reported: 'When animals use the water point, they urinate in it and worms get in it. When you drink that water,

you get parasites and a swollen body and die.' In Cherkos, Addis Ababa, there are open sewers, overflowing public toilets, and drains flooding crowded housing. The worst-off households in all sites cannot access treatment for the most basic water-related health problems such as diarrhoea.

Government health centres visited confirmed that while their supply of the most frequently needed medicines was inadequate, the poor could not afford them anyway. In all sites, stories of extremely sick people staying at home to 'pray to Allah', to 'pray to God', to 'lie on the bed and die', because they could not afford treatment, were common. In each site, health-care service providers reported that women in particular do not seek help until they are seriously ill.

The need to invest in citizenship and education

Donors are rightly concerned about good governance. The British government is committed to 'encouraging democratic structures which can hold government accountable and give the poor a voice' (DfID 1997, 30), and this has obvious implications for women.

In the Ethiopia research, it was clear that women and men had little access to decision-making bodies which formulate policy decisions affecting them. Poverty is perpetuated by a lack of access to local government and federal government structures, which are managing resources on the people's behalf. Jijiga had no form of local government structure, so neither men nor women have access to information, resources, and services. They continue to be 'governed' by default outside the formal local government system, by the all-male clan elders. A man in Belhare, Jijiga, told us: 'you won't believe this but we went to the police station to complain about having no school in the village. We did not know where to go.' Lack of access is aggravated by this lack of knowledge and by illiteracy.

Our research indicated that massive investments in basic adult, as well as primary and secondary, education and in citizenship are needed, in order to, as DfID terms it, 'give the poor a voice'. In Jijiga, men and women were equally conscious of the socially and politically crippling consequences of illiteracy: 'we want our children to be educated, not blind like us,' one man observed. The women were sure that 'if our boys went to school, they would know about the city, and they would tell the government about our problems.'

There are obvious issues here concerning gender equality. In Delanta, Metta, and Jijiga, the Orthodox Church, the mosque, and the council of Elders respectively were ranked as the most important institutions, and all are dominated by men. There were no women on school committees in Delanta or Metta. Therefore appropriate strategies to ensure women's involvement in governance and citizenship need to be encouraged while also aiming to raise the whole community's awareness. Hardly any women representatives were members of local government bodies at grassroots level, such as the *kebeles*[8] and the Peasant Associations (PA). In Metta, the PA had a women's wing, none of whose members were recruited into decision-making positions in the main PA.

Aid conditionalities, conflict, and poverty

How can development workers ensure that macro-level policies on aid and development fully respond to needs on the ground? International support is needed, including increased grant aid for human resource development and the creation of a strong civil society. Research of this kind is a first step in that it provides evidence of success or failure to do this.

In 1996, Ethiopia's external debt amounted to $10,077m, 169 per cent of its annual GNP, and more than ten times the value of its annual export earnings. Christian Aid estimates that 'for every $6

received in aid, $1 is paid straight back in debt servicing' (van Diesen and Walker 1999, 9). The IMF and World Bank policies of the 1980s and 1990s aimed to increase capacity to service debts, through emphasising the importance of export production over local economic activity. 'The IMF and World Bank can oblige [heavily indebted poor countries[9]], through conditionalities attached to loans, to redirect their macroeconomic policy in accordance with the interests of the international creditors.' These strategies have been criticised for '...maintain[ing] debtor nations in a straitjacket which prevents them from embarking upon an independent national economic policy'[10].

While improving livelihoods, citizenship, and access to basic health care and education are on the agenda, these are seriously under-resourced. Women and men in our research in Ethiopia do not want their sons and daughters to suffer as they do. In Metta, men identified 'securing the daily bread' as their main problem, and they were concerned for the 'peace and safety of their children'. They need economic, political, and social stability. They want food to give them strength to work and to go to school, they want productive livelihoods, basic medical treatments, and trained birth attendants. They want to earn sufficient cash to send their children to school clothed and fed. They need reproductive health-care education and services, clean water to reduce the incidence of disease, and are looking for support to find strategies to manage the ongoing problem of climatic change and loss of livelihoods.

In 2000, Ethiopians also face another threat to economic survival: their country is currently at war with neighbouring Eritrea. This war will inevitably reduce significantly the external resources made available to Ethiopia for achieving international human development targets. Conditions concerning 'good governance' and democracy imposed by international development funders are factors which, in a 'globalised' world, determine people's access to aid, debt relief, and, ultimately, their escape from deprivation. Western governments and international donors have an increasing tendency to withdraw from, and a reluctance to fund, countries at war. However, it is known that debt, poverty, and conflict have a cyclical relationship, and it is acknowledged that this is a cycle which needs to be broken. The British Government's International Development Select Committee (IDSC) criticised the IMF and World Bank for their approach to countries in pre- and post-conflict situations: 'The Committee notes that Rwanda's three-year adjustment programme only permits a small increase in health-care and education spending, and does not allow spending for rebuilding, reconciliation and alleviation of the "dire poverty" that was one cause of the war and genocide.' (www.jubilee2000uk.org).

Moreover, there are certain inconsistencies in international financial, industrial, and political relations, with the IMF holding centre field. Bilateral aid agreements are made with governments which may have a well documented record of human rights abuses, or may fund arms for conflicts between developing countries. The IMF agrees rescue packages with certain countries such as Indonesia and Russia, in the knowledge that this will restore confidence and trigger another round of lending by commercial banks. When probing the commitment of IMF officials to 'good governance', the IDSC found that 'it became quickly apparent that by good governance they meant primarily economic good governance, for example transparent and well-regulated financial markets, rather than human rights and participative democracy' (www.jubilee2000uk.org). This is a clear example of the many inconsistencies in the politics of development, which undermine the

likelihood of attaining human development targets and will ultimately maintain the cycle of debt, poverty, and conflict costing Africa lives and its potential.

Fra von Massow is a social development consultant and associate of the Development Planning Unit, University College, London WC1H 0PD, UK; e-mail FraVM@aol.com

Notes

1 Thanks to Peter Bourne for his comments and support.
2 These are shared targets; the Ethiopian government aims to achieve a national average primary school gross enrolment ratio of 50 per cent by 2002, and 100 per cent by 2015, and will be covering over 70 per cent of the costs of the World Bank-influenced Education Sector Development Programme.
3 The research team, also involved in producing the four site reports, included nine workers: a team leader, a senior researcher on education, a senior researcher on health, four assistant researchers, a senior statistician and an assistant and secretary.
4 We recognised that roles of women and men are not natural but socially constructed, capable of change, and context-specific. We used the term 'gender' to refer not to women or to men specifically, but to the social, economic, and political relations between them – relations in which women are often subordinate and disadvantaged. We therefore paid attention to men's roles and men's experiences of poverty as well as women's, and focused on kinship and households, since it is through these relationships and locations that gender identities and roles are reproduced.
5 Carbon debts are 'the accumulation of surplus carbon dioxide beyond the capacity of the environment to absorb' (Christian Aid 1999, 1).

6 Local flat bread.

7 Locally brewed beer made from barley or wheat.

8 Infibulation: the practice of removing the clitoris, labia minora and labia majora, stitching the girl with thorns and binding her legs until the wound heals leaving a small hole for urine and menstrual flow.

9 A local government administrative unit, which provides a link between the urban government administration and the community.

10 HIPC: heavily indebted poor countries. Under the World Bank/IMF HIPC agreements, a country has to maintain policies and repayments to the satisfaction of the IMF, while taking on board more loans to finance balance of payments deficits and structural adjustment programmes, for a minimum of three years before qualifying for debt relief. For more information, refer to the Jubilee 2000 Coalition web site: www.jubilee2000uk.org

11 Maria Clara Couto Soares of IBASE, Rio de Janeiro.

References

Christian Aid (1999) *Who Owes Who? Climate change, debt, equity and survival* Christian Aid, London.

Elson, D (1992) Male Bias in Structural Adjustment in Afshar, H (ed.) *Women and Adjustment Policies in the Third World*, Macmillan, London.

Mukangara F and Koda B (1997) *Beyond Inequalities: Women in Tanzania* TGNP/SARDC.

Pankhurst R (1998) *The Ethiopians*, Blackwell, Oxford.

Spadacini B and Nichols P (1998) 'Campaigning against female genital mutilation in Ethiopia using popular education', in *Gender and Development*, 6:2, Oxfam GB, Oxford.

UNDP Human Development Report 1999, UNDP, New York.

UNIFEM website: http://www.undp.org/unifem/economic.htm

van Diesen A and Walker C (1999) *The Changing Face of Aid to Ethiopia*, Christian Aid, London.

von Massow F (November 1999) *Oxfam Policy Department Micro Research: Health and Education in Ethiopia* (January–March 1999) unpublished report, Oxfam GB, Oxford.

The White Paper on International Development: Eliminating World Poverty: A Challenge for the 21st Century, presented to UK Parliament by the Secretary of State for International Development, 1997.

Rethinking gender and development practice for the twenty-first century[1]

Judy El-Bushra

People are confused about the concept of gender as used in development planning and practice, and male-dominated institutions are still resistant to it. This is threatening the achievement of women's rights and equality and the transformation of gender relations, argues Judy El-Bushra, and explores some definitions.

The United Nations Fourth World Conference on Women, held in Beijing in 1995, placed women's rights centre stage for governments, policy-makers, and rights workers all over the world. The Beijing conference's Platform for Action (UN 1996) has undoubtedly contributed to an increased profile for issues of gender relations in human society, and to a greater recognition of the need to overcome gender-based injustice. Governments, politicians, the media, religious movements, professional groups, and civil society generally, daily acknowledge and struggle with the implications of the global commitment to women's equality spelled out in this document.

Development agencies, in their function as an increasingly important channel for global aid transfers, have much experience to contribute to the ensuing debate. Since the publication of Esther Boserup's pioneering work on women's role in agriculture (Boserup 1970), development agencies have placed increasing emphasis on policy goals related to women in development, and this work has been well documented. From the 1970s to the 1990s, both policy and practice underwent a substantial shift from a Women in Development (WID) approach to a Gender and Development (GAD) approach (Razavi and Miller 1995), a change that has been welcomed as clarifying the essentially cultural nature of injustices which are an outcome of gender identity.

It is now 30 years since Esther Boserup first alerted the development community to the importance of women's role in agriculture, and triggered its current concern with 'gender'. My contention is that, on present evidence, GAD as a project is in danger of marginalising itself from reality, and needs a radical overhaul of its basic starting-points. Much confusion and tension exists about GAD as a concept, both within development agencies, and within institutions providing training for development agency personnel. This confusion may hinder the transformation of gender relations, and threaten the achievement of women's rights and equality. Undoubtedly, some of the confusion derives from resistance in male-dominated institutions. However, some also arises from problems with the concept of gender as we use it in development planning and practice.

The start of the twenty-first century seems a good time to acknowledge and analyse such problems, and revisit first principles, aiming to build the project of gender transformation on secure foundations for the future. This article expresses my personal views, borne out of 20 years' experience in raising the profile of gender equality and gender transformation in development agencies. Most of this experience has been with ACORD, a development agency working directly with communities in sub-Saharan Africa. I will first describe some practical difficulties I have observed in that context. The second part of the article will consider some theoretical problems in interpreting the concept of gender. The last section draws some conclusions about the challenges which gender and development practice will meet in the next phase of its evolution.

What's wrong with 'gender and development'?

In my experience, workers in development agencies — both women and men — express considerable confusion when discussing GAD in the context of their work. I see this falling into three broad areas: confusion about the discourse (what gender is about; who defines it; who is, and who is not, privileged to speak authoritatively about it); confusion about the assumption that gender transformation equals women's economic empowerment; and confusion generated by the tendency towards translating complex issues into over-simplifications and 'sloganeering'.

Confusion in the discourse

In my view, GAD tends to be seen as the realm of an exclusive group of 'gender specialists'. These 'specialists' decide who is 'gender-aware' and who is not, and what constitutes awareness. It is they who determine the content of 'gender training': a process which, it is believed, non-gender

specialists need to undergo in order to ensure that the organisation concerned is fully equipped to meet its moral and practical goals.

Unsurprisingly, different individuals and agencies differ radically in the way they interpret the concept of 'gender' in their work, each one asserting that their interpretation is correct. The word itself was used originally in linguistics. It has grown up within a European, and specifically English, tradition. It is now used in several different disciplines (including linguistics, anthropology, and, more recently, cultural studies, development studies and feminism), and its use in each of these has contributed layers of meanings. It is a word which is used in many different senses: to analyse social relations, to describe aspects of people's lives, or in judgements about the value of social change. Being a highly specialised word, it is poorly understood by the average English-speaker, and few words exist for it in other languages.

Overemphasising the economic aspect of women's empowerment

In spite of the policy shift from WID approaches to GAD approaches in the late 1980s, in practice 'gender work' is still seen first and foremost as concerning women. The fact that men too have socially-determined roles, and the social constraints on them that may exist, are addressed in token fashion if at all.[2] In much GAD work, women are treated as a homogenous category for targeting, despite the differences that may exist between them.

Both WID and GAD evolved in a policy environment dominated by economic perspectives on development, perspectives that retain their hold today. Many development agencies adopt women's economic empowerment as their main strategy for achieving gender equity, assuming that it will lead automatically to gender equality. Yet women throughout the world describe their experience of discrimination in many other areas of life, including their political roles, which define their power to control resources within social relationships, and their need for both emotional security and reproductive rights within interpersonal relationships. In relation to this last point, I have found that gender specialists often assume that women who value their relationships with male partners and relations more than their autonomy are suffering from 'false consciousness' about the nature of their oppression.

The oversimplification of complex issues

The need for agencies to formulate bite-sized 'messages' for training and lobbying purposes leads to complex issues of justice and equality being reduced to slogans. 'Two-thirds of the world's work is done by women' (UN 1985) is a typical example. This statistic is an average, abstracted from the different contexts in which development practice takes place. Used carelessly, such slogans can be highly misleading. Women's work is grindingly hard in some contexts — for example, in south-east Asia women provide up to 90 per cent of labour for rice cultivation (FAO 1999); but in others their scope for production is limited, either because of limitations placed on their opportunities outside the home, or because the economic environment is only marginally productive. (Finding viable economic niches for both women and men in stagnant economies and resource-poor environments is a challenge faced by many development agencies.) For women in such contexts, the problem may not be overwork, so much as having too little opportunity for work that would ensure their economic needs could be met. The relationship between the global picture and specific contexts where reality looks very different is extremely complex. While genuinely global statistics on gender inequalities raise awareness and are important for international activism and

advocacy work, development practice needs to be based on an understanding of the relationship between global inequality and the context-specific experiences of individual women.

The tendency in development agencies to oversimplify complex issues renders it harder to achieve solutions. An example is work to eradicate female genital mutilation (FGM). While there is no doubt that FGM is a scourge affecting millions of girls and women and their families, few successful strategies for dealing with it have emerged so far. Demonising those who practise FGM, while failing to understand the complexity of the reasons for perpetuating the practice does not reduce the incidence of FGM. Many people who practise FGM link it to the values they hold — rightly or wrongly — about gender relations, and to conceptions of beauty and purity. In some cases the practice is closely tied to cultural identity, which may explain why some refugee populations in exile maintain it more diligently than they ever did back home.[3] If FGM is to be eradicated, it will have to be addressed first and foremost at this level of emotions and attitudes, by people who understand its complexity as an issue (Toubia 1993).

Exploring the meanings of gender [4]

The question 'What is gender?' i.e. what sort of 'animal' it is, and how fundamental it is to our being, is at the root of many of the problems described above. The *Concise Oxford Dictionary* describes gender as: 'grammatical classification (or one of the classes) of objects roughly corresponding to the two sexes and sexlessness; (of nouns and pronouns) property of belonging to such class; (of adjectives) appropriate form for accompanying a noun of one such class; (colloq) one's sex' (Seventh Edition, 1982)

Gender analysis, as used by economists and social scientists, rests on a conceptual separation between gender and sex, a distinction that common speech usually

58

blurs. This separation was first spelled out in 1972 by Ann Oakley, in the following terms: 'Sex is a biological term: 'gender' a psychological and cultural one. Common sense suggests that they are merely two ways of looking at the same division and that someone who belongs to, say, the female sex will automatically belong to the corresponding (feminine) gender. In reality this is not so. To be a man or a woman, a boy or a girl, is as much a function of dress, gesture, occupation, social network and personality, as it is of possessing a particular set of genitals' (Oakley 1972, 158).

These definitions have been used by GAD trainers since the start of GAD as a field of study and work, and are usually presented as clear and unambiguous (Williams et al. 1994). However, both distinctions rest on assumptions that are increasingly being questioned.

The assumption of a distinction between male and female sexes

Is it really the case that there are two sexes — men and women — which can clearly be distinguished from each other? Observation and common sense certainly indicate that this is true in a general sense, and the science of genetics has demonstrated that there does exist a fundamental genetic difference between biological males (whose cells include an 'X' and a 'Y' chromosome) and biological females (whose cells include two 'X' chromosomes).[5] However, in the absence of genetic testing, deciding whether a person is biologically male or female largely depends on examining their external genitals, usually at birth. Not all individuals can be unambiguously identified as male and female at birth. In the United States, for example, it is accepted medical practice for individuals of indeterminate sex ('intersex' individuals) to undergo surgery during their childhood in order to assign them to one sex or the other, a practice which can be seen as a form of genital mutilation.

In addition, individuals differ from the norms, to such a significant extent that the norms themselves fail to stand up to scientific measurement. Women are commonly thought of as human beings whose vagina, womb, breasts and female hormones enable them to conceive and bear children, yet we are all aware that many people known to be 'women' are unable to bear children, because of the absence of the appropriate hormones, and sometimes the absence of, or malfunctions of, the relevant body parts. In the same way, not all men possess the necessary physical attributes to reproduce.

Finally, being born with a body characteristic of a particular sex does not guarantee that you identify with members of that sex, or even that you have to remain in the same biological sex. A proportion of individuals are 'trans-sexuals', who have the physical attributes of one sex, but lack the psychological capacity to identify with that sex. Such people often describe themselves as having been born into the 'wrong' body, and many go on in later life to live satisfying lives as a different sex after undergoing 'gender re-assignment' surgery. In many contexts, trans-sexuals become socially accepted in their new sexual identity. However, their legal position is unclear: recently, some countries have introduced, or are considering, legislation to permit trans-sexuals to be legally married in their new sex.

In summary, although physical measurement of male and female sexual characteristics is possible, in practice the identification of those characteristics is sometimes haphazard and often dependent on social convention. In many societies, there is a widespread reluctance to imagine that people could be classed in any other way than into two sexes. In some contexts, including Northern Europe and the Americas, society's desire to categorise individuals who do not conform is increasingly being considered as a human rights issue. For example, the 'third sex' movement in parts of South and North America is an informal social movement uniting trans-sexuals, intersex individuals, transvestites (people who dress as members of the opposite sex), homosexuals and others who feel they do not comfortably fit into the accepted physical confines of either of the two sexes, and who wish to campaign for a recognition of the injustice that follows. This same concern has given rise to a new sub-discipline of 'cultural studies' known as 'queer theory', which examines everything and everyone who does not fit neatly into established norms. This is discussed by Susie Jolly in her article in this issue.

The assumption of a distinction between sex and gender

GAD training also tells us that 'sex' and 'gender' are very different ways of classifying human beings. How true is this? Does 'sex' really belong only to the realm of empirically observable science, and 'gender' only to the realm of culture? There seem to be three sorts of arguments that this may not be the case. First is the argument that sexual distinctions are themselves part of culture. What we regard as characteristic of 'sex' includes many different elements of human nature rolled into one. Foucault (1978) put it in this way: '...the notion of 'sex' made it possible to group together, in an artificial unity, anatomical elements, biological functions, conducts, sensations, and pleasures, and it enabled one to make use of this fictitious unity as a causal principle, an omnipresent meaning' (Foucault 1978, 154).

Secondly, views of biological sex common in the West are not necessarily shared by others. Moore (1994) refers to studies from Nepal and Papua New Guinea, where it is believed that the biological characteristics of male and female may both exist within one body, may be exchanged during eating or sexual

intercourse, or may change during the course of a person's lifetime. For example, 'in Nepal ... the differences between the female and the male are conceived of as the difference between flesh and bone. However, these differences of gender are said to be located in all bodies, thus collapsing the distinction between sexed bodies and socially constructed genders ... The female and the male, as flesh and bone, are necessary features of [everyone's] bodily identity.' (Moore 1994, 13)

There is a second debate which needs to be had about the distinction between sex and gender that we use in GAD. This is rather different. It focuses on research in other disciplines that raises questions about whether the 'gender differences' we associate with women and men are socially constructed, or whether they are in fact genetic. We must now question whether male and female social behaviour is entirely learned, or whether some of it is determined by inherited factors. Modern evolutionary theory argues that human sexual behaviour, as well as the human body, has developed from generation to generation, to ensure the 'reproduction of the fittest'. In this view, the survival of the human race is best served by individual men and women aiming to reproduce themselves through having children, who are conceived and nurtured to maturity in the greatest numbers and in the best possible conditions. Everyday human behaviour is driven by this need, which affects different people in different ways. Thus, differences in behaviour between men and women, and even between rich and poor, royalty and commoners, hill-dwellers and desert people, can be explained by differences in their reproductive strategies. In this argument, culture is derived from biology, not the other way round (Ridley 1993).

Moreover, biologists have now gone a long way in mapping human genes; genes have been discovered that govern or affect a number of areas of human behaviour, previously believed to depend on individual choices or socialisation. According to this research, whether girls play with dolls or with toy motorbikes depends partly on how they are brought up, but also on tendencies that are part of their sex-related genetic inheritance. This links to research nearly half a century ago in linguistics. Noam Chomsky pioneered the view that children are born with innate knowledge, not of any particular language as such, but of the basic ground-rules of language structures (Chomsky 1957). This may also lend support to the idea that some form of predisposition towards a 'gender identity' is at least a possibility. The arguments put forward by geneticists and linguists are not proven, and all are the subject of controversy; there are no definitive answers.

All in all, Ann Oakley's definition of gender seems to be a simple statement of reality, and it has become fundamental to GAD work. Many of our current assumptions about men and women in society are based on it. However, there is now evidence suggesting that the concepts we use are nothing like as clear and unambiguous as they first seemed. 'Men' and 'women', 'male' and 'female', 'sex' and 'gender' are all words surrounded by controversy, and are subject to complex and different interpretations.

Moreover, we seem to be fixated by the need to describe the world in terms of a whole series of polar opposites. Might there not be intermediate or overlapping categories, which would better represent the complexity of real life?

Some implications

Eternal vigilance is needed as we work to promote gender equality and justice.

I do not think that the above discussion should lead us to conclude that differences between the sexes are unimportant, nor should it undermine our view that the oppression of women is one of the major issues of our time. Women are widely discriminated against in their personal lives, in their economic opportunities, in their opportunities for political and creative expression, and in the area of legal rights. Their life choices are relatively restricted, especially if they are caring for children, and their vulnerability to domestic and other violence is high.

However, what the foregoing does imply is that we may well be oversimplifying the issues, and that we can best understand women's position in the context of a more nuanced and sophisticated understanding of the roots of human behaviour. If we are concerned about oppression, marginalisation and injustice, we need to recognise that these are features of all human societies, and that they are linked to a variety of factors of which difference between the sexes is just one. As Henrietta Moore puts it, 'When has gender ever been pure, untainted by other forms of difference, other relations of inequality? Lives are shaped by a multiplicity of differences.... The concepts of sexual difference and gender difference collide at this moment and cannot usefully be separated again.... And as for gender discourse, there is no discourse on gender outside the discourses of race and class and ethnicity and sexuality and so on' (Moore 1994, 20).

We need to move beyond the neat distinctions between 'sex' and 'gender' and 'men' and 'women' used in development agencies, to develop a theory of social relations that enables us to understand the way in which our identities are rooted in our physical bodies on the one hand, and in our historical context on the other.

Here are three elements of such a theory which are indicated by the above argument. First, we need to envisage social relations themselves as the mainframe of analysis, looking at the totality of the elements in our identities and our interactions with others as the starting-point. From here, we need to understand the standpoints of various individuals within this system. The 'social relations framework', developed at the Institute of Development Studies, UK (Kabeer 1994), accepts the 'inter-connectedness' of men's and women's roles, and seeks to understand the 'relations of everyday life' in the context of the institutional underpinnings of gender hierarchy. Institutions need to be 'unpacked', so that we can understand how they function in terms of rules, resources, people, activities and power structures. A key part of this understanding is that institutions are not monolithic structures: they are constantly being re-created, through the struggles of women and men to define their own ideas of equality and empowerment and create a viable and satisfying life for themselves in the context of — or in spite of — their social identities.

Gender should not be seen — as it sometimes is in development agencies — as *the* major axis of social differentiation. Rather, we should understand people's experience of gender differentiation as linked to their experience of other forms of social difference, such as those of age, race or class. This understanding of people's identities as complex and nuanced permits a closer understanding of power relations in general, and the illumination of contra-dictions and injustices inherent in those relations. GAD specialists should draw on sociological work on the nature of power, including feminist interpretations which delve into the varied forms of power that women and men have imposed on them and that they themselves wield. For example, Bob Connell uses such nuanced definitions of power to develop the notion of 'hegemonic masculinity' to describe the subordination of men to men as an aspect of patriarchal power relations (Connell 1995).

Finally, development agencies and the academic world alike have generally been slow — and reluctant? — to acknowledge the relevance of homosexual experience to an understanding of gender identities and gendered patterns of oppression. I have found in my work that it is widely assumed that same-sex relations are a feature of the so-called advanced capitalist world, and therefore not relevant to development. In particular, homosexuality is seen as a 'luxury' issue in environments of extreme poverty. This ignores the fact that what has changed in the 'West' is the degree of openness about homosexuality, and therefore the possiblity of living it, rather than the desire to live it. In any environment, suppression of sexuality has the potential to lead to untold social problems, as well as personal unhappiness. The lack of attention to homosexual experience is a pity, since attitudes towards sexuality may offer important insights into the nature of gender identities and gender oppression generally,[6] and assist GAD practitioners in exposing the gender stereotyping that is at the root of gender inequality and injustice.

Moreover, to the extent that develop-ment agencies lack interest in human sexuality, this may also reflect a lack of concern over reproductive health and sexual relations generally. Indeed, the whole area of interpersonal relations and emotional life constitutes a major blind spot in dominant development paradigms.

Conclusions

'Gender' should be seen not as a politically correct ideology, but as an integral element in a wider search for a deep understanding of human behaviour, which concerns itself with physical and emotional needs, perceptions, motivations, relationships and structures. Concepts such as 'identity', 'agency' and 'power' describe how human beings struggle to carve out acceptable lives for themselves in the constraints imposed by their historical positions, their social roles, and their personal attributes. If the concept of gender is to be a useful tool for development and for the advancement of women's rights, GAD research, policy and practice must direct its energies towards understanding the complex meanings of this and similar concepts, and resist promoting itself as an unquestionable good.

Judy El-Bushra is Acting Director of the Research and Policy Programme at ACORD, 52 Horseferry Road, London SW1P 2AF, UK. Telephone: +44 (0)20 7227 8628; e-mail: judye@acord.org.uk

References

Butler, J (1990) *Gender Trouble: Feminism and the subversion of identity*, Routledge, London.

Connell, B (1995) *Masculinities*, Polity Press, Cambridge.

El-Bushra, J 'Transforming conflict: some thoughts on a gendered understanding of conflict processes' in Jacobs, S et al. (eds) (forthcoming), *States of Violence: Gender, violence and resistance*, Zed Press, London.

Elshtain, JB (1992) 'The power and powerlessness of women', in Bock and James (eds) (1992) *Beyond Equality and Difference: Citizenship, feminist politics and female subjectivity*, Routledge, London.

Foucault, M (1978) *The History of Sexuality*, Vol. 1, Penguin Books, UK.

Dunne B (1998) 'Power and sexuality in the Middle East', Middle East Research and Information Project (MERIP); website: http://www.merip.org

Kabeer, N (1994) *Reversed Realities: Gender hierarchies in development thought*, Verso, London.

Moore, H (1994) *A Passion for Difference*, Polity Press, Cambridge.

Oakley (1972) *Sex, Gender and Society*, Temple Smith.

Razavi, S and Miller, C (1995) *From WID to GAD: Conceptual shifts in the women and development discourse*, UNRISD.

Ridley, M (1993) *The Red Queen: Sex and the evolution of human nature*, Penguin Books, UK.

Toubia, N (1993) *Female Genital Mutilation: A call for action*, Women, Ink.

UN Department of Public Information (1996), *Platform for Action and the Beijing Declaration*, New York.

Notes

1 Based on a paper presented to a conference on 'NGOs in a global future' at the University of Birmingham, January 1999.

2 It is only fairly recently that 'masculinity' has become a major issue in the academic field, giving rise, for example to a series of seminars in the UK funded by the Economic and Social Research Council. The debate about masculinity and its place in gender studies in the development field is still young.

3 Health workers among the Somali community in the UK, for example, report hardened attitudes towards FGM, although the custom had been beginning to lose ground during the Siyad Barre regime (personal communication, Halimo Hersi, 1990).

4 Henrietta Moore, in *A Passion for Difference*, inspired much of this section (Moore 1994).

5 For a summary of current research in genetics, see Ridley, M (1993).

6 For example, B Dunne describes how Middle Eastern attitudes towards male homosexuals mirror those of men towards women (Dunne1998).

'Put your money where your mouth is!': The need for public investment in women's organisations

Siobhan Riordan

If we are to attain gender equality in the twenty-first century, the organisations which carry forward this agenda must be strengthened. This article explores the inadequate funding of women's organisations[1] by governments and donors, gives examples of their contribution to political processes, and argues that the political rhetoric of supporting women's organisations must be turned into reality.

Throughout the twentieth century, women have created organisations that seek to improve the status and situation of women. Around the world, these have often been the driving force behind social change (Perlmutter 1994, Walter 1998). By the end of the century, political rhetoric had begun to acknowledge their role in achieving gender equality; calls have come from all quarters — including the World Bank, the United Nations, the European Union, international NGOs, national and local government — for partnership between 'mainstream' organisations and women's organisations, in order to advance social and economic development.

In particular, women's organisations were identified as key stakeholders in achieving the UN Global Platform for Action, agreed at Beijing in 1995. Paragraph 298 of the Platform for Action states: 'Non-governmental organisations should be encouraged to contribute to the design and implementation of these strategies or national plans of action. They should also be encouraged to develop their own programmes to complement government efforts. Women's organisations and feminist groups, in collaboration with other non-governmental organisations, should be encouraged to organise networks, as necessary, and to advocate for and support the implementation of the Platform for Action by governments and regional and international bodies' (DfEE, undated, 41).

What hinders or supports women's organisations?

First, the political context in which women's organisations operate raises issues such as the availability of resources to NGOs, and the difficulty or ease of accessing them; women's status in society; political agendas; the kinds of public institutions which exist, and their mandates and agendas; and civil rights within a particular context. All these affect the capacity of women's organisations to operate effectively.

Another group of factors relates to the historical context in which women's organisations are operating. Issues here include the values and principles of different women's movements, a particular organisation's stage of development, as well as the stage of development of wider social movements in that context.

A third group of factors affecting the progress of women's organisations relate to the organisation itself. Issues here include the dynamics of power between women in the organisation, which are linked to those in wider society; the organisational structure, leadership, and management style; the balance between paid and unpaid workers; and the ownership and control of the organisation.

This article focuses on one issue within the political context: the availability of, and access to, financial and technical resources. It should be noted at the outset that I do not seek to argue that all women's organisations *should* be funded by the state and public donors; many choose not to take this path for fears of co-optation or constraints on their work. However, for those organisations which choose to, or need to, engage with the state and donors in order to secure sufficient resources to achieve their goals, then the choice needs to be available. At present, there is growing evidence from across the world that many women's organisations do not have this choice.

The research

The research on which this article is based came about because of a wish to understand why so many women's organisations in the UK exist on the margins of viability, with dilapidated offices, out-of-date equipment, poorly paid (if at all) workers, and inadequate funds. I found that a significant determinant of the development of women's organisations in the UK is their ability to command resources and secure public funding from state and donor agencies. Inadequate resources and the current allocation of public funds undermine the capacity of British women's organisations to respond to the social, political, and economic problems they seek to address. Funding plans that specifically target initiatives promoting women's equality can help to ensure that public funds reach women's organisations, thereby strengthening their capacity to achieve their goals.

The research took place between 1996 and 1999 and used a range of methods, including ten in-depth interviews with women working paid and unpaid in women's organisations (Riordan 1998b); 30 interviews with 'key informants', women and men who were selected for their first-hand knowledge about this topic; archival analysis of policy-makers' and funders' public records and reports (Riordan 1998c); and a gender analysis of records of public funds disbursed to British non-government organisations (Riordan 1998a).

Women's agendas and organisations

Researchers into organisational development argue that the needs and aspirations of human beings are the reasons for organised effort in society (French and Bell 1978). Thus, women's organisations are specific sites for the articulation of women's needs, and the application of women's solutions (Iannello 1992; Young et al. 1993).

The scope and range of women's organisations around the globe at the start of the twenty-first century is an impressive testimony to women's organising efforts, and demonstrates the diversity of women's agendas. Thousands of diverse women's groups and organisations have emerged in the past 20 years, across Latin America, Africa, Asia and the Middle East, as well as in Europe and North America (Karl 1995; Perlmutter 1994; Sen and Grown 1987; Wallace and March 1991). A European study of seven countries concluded that women's shared agenda made them the 'driving force in local action' (EFILWC 1992, 86). While some organisations are explicitly feminist in aim, others do not identify themselves as part of a women's movement, but nevertheless address concerns related to women's practical needs, in health care, law, child care, education, and employment legislation (Coward 1994, 13).

One interviewee in my UK research explained the considerable impact of women's organisations on her context: 'A lot of women's organisations came out of unfunded activist groupings in the 1960s and 1970s, and I think they are admirable. They have changed the face of social service provision. They have raised the issue of domestic violence and preventative health care. They have transformed the way many issues are dealt with in society, the way that domestic violence has been recognised. Until three or four years ago, there was no such thing as rape in marriage. It has been the work of those organisations which has changed the whole spectrum of society.'

Despite this success, lack of adequate funding hampers the capacity of women's organisations in the UK, and elsewhere, to influence and shape political and economic agendas. Despite their diversity of context and aim, women's agendas have one thing in common: they remain marginalised by power structures.

The failure of social policy to address women's priorities

Much research in a range of Northern and Southern contexts has indicated that women's social, economic, political, and personal agendas fail to be represented in the economic and political power structures which govern society (Sen and Grown 1987; Stein 1997; Women's Communication Centre (WCC) 1996, 1997). Evidence of this gulf between women's agendas and political power structures can be found across the world's regions. Created and controlled by a shrinking elite of men, political and economic power structures are concerned with a development model of unlimited growth of goods and services, of money revenue, of technological progress, and of a concept of well-being identified as an abundance of industrially produced commodities (Mies 1997).

In contrast, feminists have long argued that women's caring roles and their responsibilities in society produce different priorities, concerns, and needs to the predominantly male elite who control economic globalisation and govern political power structures. In June 1995, in the UK, women's different agendas were articulated through the largest ever survey of women's attitudes, concerns and policy agendas. In June 1995, 10,000 women were asked, 'what do you want?'; this survey generated 46,000 'wants', and the authors concluded that the findings show the need for a radical re-evaluation of how we think about women, their concerns, and their approaches to the social and economic problems of our time (WCC 1996). The researchers concluded that if the solutions offered by women in the survey were adopted, it would lead to a fundamental shift in political priorities, political process, and political culture (WCC 1996, 9).

In a study across seven European countries, it was found that concern about the care, health, and education of children was a shared concern provoking local action, and common to all countries, although the pattern of constraints varies considerably according to national and local conditions (EFILWC 1992). Women are ultimately responsible for the daily survival and care of children, the elderly, the sick, and disabled in the community. For some, there is a clear connection between men's isolation from direct caring roles and their violent exploitation of not only women, but the environment and the 'Third World' (Mies 1986).

Research in many contexts has indicated that, in addition to having different agendas, women's organisations demonstrate different values: co-operation, an emphasis on relatedness, the inclusion of the personal dimension, valuing feeling and giving status to intuition, and commitment to taking a long-term perspective rather than pursuing short-term gains (Page 1997;

Yasmin 1997; Stewart and Taylor 1997). The fact that women organise points not only to the connections between economic, political and social needs, but to the need for an approach to organisational development which promotes social cohesion.

Women's agendas in action

An example of the difference in agendas between women in the community, and political and economic leaders who control resources and determine the priorities of public policy, comes from a comparison of women's peace-building efforts in Northern Ireland, Israel, and Bosnia. In her research on this subject, Cynthia Cockburn (1996) discovered that women had created grassroots organisations which were valid peace-building processes in their own right. They provided institutional models for peace-building and laid the foundations for co-operation between people divided by ethnicity, religion, and political affiliation. Arab women organised with Jewish women, Catholic women with Protestant women, and Muslim, Croat, Bosnian, and Serb women organised together. In these areas of explosive conflict, other civil society organisations have failed to generate, or failed to sustain, ethnic mixing, yet women have succeeded in transcending ethnic and religious divides in working to improve the situation and status of women in their communities, and their ability to sustain the lives of their dependents and communities.

However, as Cockburn concludes in her research, there is a great gulf between such small-scale women's initiatives and the power structures in which cease-fires are agreed and constitutions negotiated. Women in all the projects she examines point out that while they often prepare the groundwork for peace, they are neither present nor acknowledged when male leaders make (and break) peace agreements. Women may have different perceptions from men of what is needed, and male bias in political institutions results in women's priorities being excluded within public and development policy which determines the allocation of funds (ibid.).

Public funding and women's organisations

One of the critical factors that maintains the gulf between women's agendas and political power structures is inadequate public investment in women's organisations (Riseborough 1997; Clarke 1998). Without economic and decision-making power, women's organisations are dependent on others for resources. And if those resources are not forthcoming, this undermines the capacity of organisations to promote women's agendas.

Nowhere is this argument more aptly demonstrated than in Northern Ireland. The Northern Ireland Women's Coalition (NIWC) was formed in 1996 to contest the elections to the multi-party peace talks. The NICW won 1 per cent of the vote but two seats at the talks. Northern Ireland does not have a single woman MP in the UK parliament or the European parliament, and only 14 per cent of local councillors are women. The Coalition argues that this lack of political representation is a direct result of a society dominated by militarism and nationalism, set against a background of violence. Since the political space left for women is very small, they tend to be active in community, rather than formal, politics. The Coalition grew out of this community activism, helping women to move from community politics to a more formal arena (Clarke 1998).

The NIWC's impact can be seen throughout the Good Friday Peace Agreement, which the people of Northern Ireland voted to accept on 22 May 1998. The 'women's agenda' which the Coalition brought to the peace talks resulted in commitments to equal opportunity and to safeguards for the human rights and religious liberties of all sections of the community. The setting up of the new Civic Forum, included in the agreement, provides people from outside political life (representatives of the private sector, trades union and voluntary sectors) with the opportunity to be consulted on political questions. The creation of the Forum was a specific proposal which the NIWC brought to the peace-talks, and the women concluded that their involvement made a real difference to the final agreement: 'You can see our values and ideas throughout the document: in the proposal for the Civic Forum, in the consideration of the victims of violence and in the explicit right given to women to equal political participation' (ibid., 8).

Yet, in spite of this success in bringing women's agendas into the peace-making and political process, NIWC was forced to make a plea for funds to sustain its work in the summer of 1998. The Coalition has fought five elections in two years, relying on individual donations and membership subscriptions. Monica McWilliams (one of two candidates recently elected to the newly formed National Assembly) argued that without an additional £10,000, the Coalition would be unable to continue, and women's agendas could be lost in the National Assembly of Northern Ireland, especially given that only 14 out of 122 Assembly Members are women (ibid.).

Papering over the cracks

The role of women's organisations is explicitly stated in those paragraphs of the Beijing Platform for Action which list strategic objectives and actions. If this rhetoric about women's equality is to become a reality, beyond the Beijing Plus Five meetings in Washington later this year, then it requires investment.

Despite calls to integrate women's organisations into economic and social development, I found considerable evidence to suggest that they experience obstacles in accessing financial resources. Even where there is political rhetoric about women's equality, this invariably fails to be matched by public investment in women's equality initiatives (Goetz 1997; Kardam 1997) or organisations working to this agenda.

Interestingly, I was able to find very little literature which has examined and analysed the funding of women's organisations. Literature about women's organisations, both in countries of the South and the North, constantly makes reference to inadequate funding undermining the effectiveness of women's organisations; however, it does not usually analyse this situation any further (del Rosario 1997; Griffin 1995, 7). However, the primary research confirmed that women's organisations face the problems of insufficient funds, understaffing, and marginality to mainstream economic and social development. This, in turn, undermines organisational development and capacity to influence political agendas and development policy. As one interviewee in the research explained: 'Getting more of a commitment from those with resources to target women's organisations would enable so much more to happen. Working from desperation and survival is not a powerful place to be; … [you're] doing things half-baked. You're papering over cracks. That's how it is when you're working with desperation and survival.'

This is a particularly familiar picture for those organisations which combine both practical and strategic responses to women's needs — the very approach needed to make political rhetoric a reality. In the context of international development, Caroline Moser observed almost ten years ago that, because the work which genuinely seeks to empower the powerless is potentially challenging to those in power, women's organisations which aim to empower women remain largely unsupported both by national governments and bilateral aid agencies. They are underfunded, reliant on the use of voluntary and unpaid women's time, and dependent on the resources of those few international non-government agencies and First World governments prepared to support this approach to women and development (Moser 1991b).

In both UK policy and in international development, there is some evidence that public funds are available for meeting the practical needs of women (Margetts 1996; Newman and Williams 1995; Stewart and Taylor 1997). However, there is little to show that public funds are available for responding to women's strategic needs (Griffin 1995).

Monitoring public investment

While the UK's socio-political context is unique, there are some lessons to be learned from this research which may be of relevance to women in other contexts. If political rhetoric about women's equality, be it at a local, regional, national, or international level, is to become a reality, then investment of public resources is necessary.

Given the current situation for women's organisations, with evidence from across the world of under-investment and inadequate funding, it is now necessary to devise systems for monitoring public expenditure to women's organisations. Without such systems, it will remain difficult to expose the inadequacy of funding and resources, and the emptiness of political rhetoric. At the University of East London, we have received three years' funding to develop a scheme for monitoring public funds to women's organisations in the UK (Riordan 1998a and 1998b). As part of an ongoing research programme, we will be examining the often innovative and creative strategies women's organisations pursue to generate resources, while maintaining their autonomy and independence from state and donor control.

Public investment in women's organisations needs to be monitored at a local, national, and international level, as well as within donor agencies and domestic foundations. Such monitoring could provide important evidence to influence and shape development agendas and public policy priorities. It offers an opportunity to call political and economic leaders to account. More importantly, it provides a tool to expose the inadequacy of public investment in the organisations created by women to find solutions for the problems of our time.

Siobhan Riordan is a Visiting Research Fellow at the Centre for Institutional Studies, University of East London, Manbey Park Road, London E15 1EY, UK; she also works as an independent management consultant to NGOs. E-mail: siobhan@ndirect.co.uk

Note

1 Women's organisations are here defined as those run by and for women, and which seek to improve the status and situation of women.

References

Black, N (1989) *Social Feminism*, Cornell University Press, Ithaca, USA.

Brown (1992) *Women Organising*, Routledge, London.

Chatterjee, M (1993) 'Struggle and development: Changing the reality of self- employed workers' in Young G et al. (eds) (1993).

Clarke (1998) 'More Talk?', in *Sibyl* July/August, Agender Ltd, London.

Cockburn, C (1996) 'Missing It', in *Red Pepper*, September.

Coote, A and Campbell, B (1987) *Sweet Freedom: The struggle for women's liberation*, 2nd Edition, Blackwell, Oxford.

del Rosario, VO (1997) 'Mainstreaming gender concerns: Aspects of compliance, resistance and negotiation' in Goetz AM (ed) (1997).

DfEE (Undated) 'Fourth United Nations World Conference on Women - Platform for Action: Report of Consultation Exercise', Sex and Race Equality Division, Department for Education and Employment, London.

Doyal, L (1995) *What Makes Women Sick? Gender and the political economy of health*, Macmillan, London.

EFILWC (1992) 'Out of the shadows: Local community action and the European Community', European Foundation for the Improvement of Living and Working Conditions, Dublin, Ireland.

French, WL and Bell Jr., CH (1978) *Organisation Development: Behaviour science interventions for organisation improvement*, Prentice-Hall Inc., New Jersey, USA.

Goetz, AM (ed) (1997) *Getting Institutions Right for Women in Development*, Zed Books, London.

Griffin, G (ed) *Feminist Activism in the 1990s*, Taylor Francis, London.

Iannello, KP (1992) *Decisions without Hierarchy: Feminist interventions in organisation theory and practice*, Routledge, London.

Itzin, C and Newman, J (eds) (1995) *Gender, Culture and Organizational Change: Putting theory in practice*, Routledge, London.

Kardam, N (1997) 'Making development organizations accountable: The organizational, political and cognitive contexts' in Goetz AM (ed) (1997).

Karl M, (1995) *Women and Empowerment: Participation and decision making*, Zed Press, London.

Kooiman, J (ed) (1993) *Modern Governance: New government-society interactions*, Sage Publications, London.

Kuppers, G (ed) (1992) *Companeras: Voices from the Latin American women's movement*, Latin American Bureau, Russell Press, Nottingham.

Margetts, H (1996) 'Public Management Change and Sex Equality within the State' in Lovenduski J and Norris P (eds)

Women in Politics, Oxford University Press.

Mies, M (1986) *Patriarchy and Accumulation on a World Scale: Women in the international division of labour*, Zed Books, London.

Mies, M (1997) 'Do we need a new "moral economy?"', in *Canadian Woman Studies: Bridging North and South - Patterns of Transformation*, Spring 1997, 17:2, Inanna Publications and Education Inc., Toronto, Canada.

Moser, C (1991a) 'Gender planning in the Third World: Meeting practical and strategic needs' in Grant, R and Newland, K (eds) *Gender and International Relations*, Open University Press, Milton Keynes.

Moser, C (1991b) 'Gender planning in the Third World' in Wallace T and March C (eds) (1991).

Mosse, JC (1993) *Half the World, Half a Chance: An introduction to gender and development*, Oxfam Publications, Oxford.

Newland, K (1991) 'From transnational relationships to international relations: Women in development and the international decade for women', in Grant R and Newland K (eds) *Gender and International Relations*, Open University Press, Milton Keynes.

Newman, J and Williams, F (1995) 'Diversity and change: Gender, welfare and organizational relations' in Itzin C and Newman J (eds) (1995).

ODA (1989) 'Women, development and the British aid programme: A progress report', Overseas Development Administration, London.

ODA (1993) *Social Development Handbook: A guide to social issues in ODA projects and programmes*, Overseas Development Administration, London.

Page, M (1997) *Women in Beijing, One Year On: Networks, alliances, coalitions*, Community Development Foundation Publications, London.

Perlmutter, FD (ed) (1994) *Women and Social Change: Non-profit and social policy,*

National Association of Social Workers, Washington, USA.

Riordan, S (1998a) 'Organisations of the women's movement: Countering invisibility' in *Dimensions of the Voluntary Sector: Key facts, figures, analysis and trends* (1998) Charities Aid Foundation, Kent.

Riordan, S (1998b) 'Women's organisations in the UK voluntary sector: A force for social change', Centre for Institutional Studies, University of East London.

Riordan, S (1998c) 'Women's organisations and public resources' in 'Are Women Getting Their Fair Share of the Resources?', a Women's Resource Centre seminar report, April, WRC, London.

Riseborough, M (1997) 'The gender report: Women and regional regeneration in the Midlands', Centre for Urban and Regional Studies, School of Public Policy, University of Birmingham.

Rose, K (1992) *Where Women are Leaders: The SEWA movement in India*, Zed Books, London.

Rothschild, J (1991) 'Towards a feminine model of organization', working paper, quoted in Robbins SP (1993) *Organisational Behaviour: Concepts, controversies and applications*, Prentice Hall International, New Jersey, USA.

Sen, G and Grown, C (1987) *Development, Crises, and Alternative Visions: Third World women's perspectives*, New Feminist Library, Monthly Review Press, New York, USA.

Shiva, V (1988) *Staying Alive: Women Ecology, and Survival in India*, Kali for Women, Delhi, India.

Shiva, V (1997) 'Economic Globalization, Ecological Feminism, and Sustainable Development' in *Canadian Woman Studies: Bridging North and South - Patterns of Transformation*, Spring 1997, 17: 2, Inanna Publications and Education Inc., Toronto, Canada.

Stein, J (1997) *Empowerment and Women's Health: Theory, methods and practice*, Zed Books, London.

Stewart, S and Taylor, J (1997) 'Women organizing women: "Doing it backwards and in high heels"', in Goetz AM (ed) (1997).

Wallace, T and March, C (eds) (1991) *Changing Perceptions: Writings on gender and development*, Oxfam GB, Oxford.

White, J (1995) 'Leading in their own ways: Women chief executives in local government', in Itzin C and Newman J (eds) (1995).

Women's Communication Centre (1996) *Values and Visions: The report from the What Women Want social survey*, WCC, London.

Yasmin, T (1997) 'What is Different about Women's Organizations?' in Goetz AM (ed) (1997).

Young, G, Samarsinghe, V and Kusterer, K (eds) (1993) *Women at the Center: Development issues and practices for the 1990s*, Kumarian Press, Connecticut, USA.

Culture as a barrier to rural women's entrepreneurship:
Experience from Zimbabwe

Colletah Chitsike

Gender analysis shows that women can only be self-confident and autonomous in their economic activities if no cultural restraints hold them back. This article identifies the most important issues to be addressed by programmes and projects aiming to promote women's equality through entrepreneurship and makes suggestions for the future focus of gender programmes, especially training.

In 2000, millions of women throughout the developing world (including my home country, Zimbabwe) continue to experience problems related to lack of money, resources and economic power. As a gender and development consultant, I am increasingly being asked to facilitate the planning of programmes that aim to train women entrepreneurs to gain self confidence and autonomy in enterprise management. In this article, I explore ideas of entrepreneurship, and highlight the reasons why a gender analysis of women's context must underpin attempts to promote women entrepreneurs. The current interest in finding ways of enhancing women's capacity does not necessarily indicate that development organisations are acknowledging the cultural and structural barriers to becoming entrepreneurs that women face — and that the concept of entrepreneurship is itself biased towards men.

Entrepreneurship as a gendered concept

In the last three decades of the twentieth century, pressure on national governments to end women's poverty came from all levels of society: from the United Nations, through the Platforms of Action that have come from global conventions, to community organisations representing women in countries worldwide. In all these, as in development funding organisations and governments, the goal of women's 'economic empowerment' has been the focus of many lengthy discussions, and much analysis. In practice, these discussions have tended to result in various kinds of income-generating projects for women (with emphasis on those from rural areas). From the 1980s, in line with dominant neo-liberal ideas of promoting economic growth through individual effort, the terminology used has been of promoting women's 'entrepreneurship'.

The word 'entrepreneur' is defined by the *Oxford Complete Wordfinder* as a 'person who undertakes an enterprise or business with the chance of profit or loss, person in control of a commercial undertaking, a contractor acting as an intermediary' (Tulloch 1993). Other words that the wordfinder suggests as close approximations are 'adventurer', 'intermediary' and 'executive'. Although this definition of entrepreneurship seems straightforward and gender-neutral, and may be understood as such by some programme planners, in fact there is evidence from programme evaluations that the social context in which women and men live influences their ability to become entrepreneurs.

An example comes from my own experience in the early 1990s, when the International Labour Organisation (ILO) undertook a project in Zambia, Zimbabwe and Uganda. It aimed to produce Start Your Business [SYB] training manuals and to train trainers, who, in turn, would train potential women entrepreneurs. When the ILO project was later evaluated, a key finding was that training that emphasises business training alone does not guarantee successful entrepreneurship. In addition, a gender analysis of the processes and sorts of behaviour that are important in entrepreneurship is needed, and training materials should be developed that meet women's needs. In the ILO project, potential entrepreneurs in all three countries had had not only to overcome the generally unfavourable macroeconomic environment, but additional structural barriers that face women specifically. These included lower levels of education than men, and a much more limited availability of finance for start-up capital. Women in all three countries also have to overcome cultural constraints, in societies that do not encourage them to behave in an entrepreneurial manner (ILO internal report 1997).

While structural barriers are clearer than cultural ones, and may be more easily overcome, the two types of barriers are subtly linked. A good example of a structural barrier that has been changed in Zimbabwe is the 1981 establishment of a legal age of majority for all. Previously, women were regarded as minors. However, although the law now recognises women as adults, cultural barriers still exist, that deny women use of this law. In any southern African country, women running a small business in an isolated village face different structural barriers from those in a city; but similar cultural barriers are identified as problems by women in both village and city. These are at the root of women's marginalisation from economic, political and social resources, and their heavy, dual workload of family caring as well as production.

Cultural barriers

Cultural barriers to women entrepreneurs, which I have seen in my work in Zimbabwe and elsewhere, lie in the difference in the way that women and men view entrepreneurship as a concept. I discussed the topic of women, men and money with women during workshops for Project Making Sense, a communications project to explain entrepreneurship, in 1998. The women's attitudes can be characterised as follows. For some women, making large amounts of money is a dirty pursuit, full of all kinds of evil. In Zimbabwe, women are traditionally brought up to associate making money with immorality: the Shona expression *anoda mari sehure* ('she wants to make money like a prostitute') expresses utmost disgust. The predominant male view of business is that one has to acquisitive and assertive — perhaps even ruthless — to be a success. Even where a positive aspect is recognised the titles given to women who are strong and decisive are based on male standards. For example, in one of the Shona dialects, the term *bambo mukunda* (father-daughter) refers to a daughter who takes male responsibilities. The language fails to acknowledge the female gender, and lacks words that express the strengths of women.

During a field workshop in Gwanda, Zimbabwe, for the same intervention, I was told about women who are involved in gold-mining. They restrict their involvement to panning for gold, which requires basic equipment and no skills. It is men who do the larger-scale panning, and access heavy machinery to mine. Women tend to depend on selling their gold to middle-men. This is a hazardous process (*zvevanhu vemadhiri*), involving shady deals. During the severe drought of 1992, a woman who had panned a large piece of gold approached a middle-man to sell it for her. She received only Z$4,000 (US$100) for it; in her presence, the middle-man sold the same piece to a tourist who was passing by, and received Z$30,000 (US$1,000) for it. When the woman tried to argue with the middle man to get a fair share of the fee, she was told that she had sold the piece and the contract had been agreed upon. When she continued to argue, she was threatened.

The belief that women cannot run large-scale businesses leads some to pretend that men are involved in order to conform to cultural expectations. During a workshop for self-awareness for widows run by Harare Anglican Diocese Mothers' Union, I heard of a woman who ran a lucrative and very productive commercial farm. Her husband had been imprisoned soon after they purchased the farm, and she ran their agricultural business in a very successful manner. When her husband died, however, this woman proceeded to invite her brother to come to live on the farm. Asked why she did this, she responded that she had to have a male live on the farm as protection from her late husband's family, and that her family could not allow her to own the success. She explained that, according to her culture, she owed her success to her ancestors and therefore she needed the male relative to be present to own that success. The mixing of traditional cultural beliefs and the skills of entrepreneurship is an area that needs investigation and research.

In summary, women are permitted to want money, but not large sums of money. When they have it, they have to hide the fact, neither showing it nor claiming that they have earned it due to personal success: instead, they say *ndeya baba*, ('it belongs to father/husband'). In traditional custom, everything that belongs to a married

woman in Zimbabwe actually belongs to her husband; he has the right to own her through *lobola* (the bride price paid by the future husband to the bride's parents). In customary law women do not have individual economic rights, on the grounds that they have benefits given to them through their spouses or male relatives. The women in the Project Making Sense workshops felt that money is an expression of power, and that culture is used by men as a way to keep women distanced from power. They said that in contrast to those associated with money-making (and men), the social qualities associated with women in Shona society include skills in fostering peace and preventing conflict; fairness and equity in distributing resources so that society and the family benefit (even to the extent of denying themselves resources for the benefit of others); and the promotion of social justice and reduction in exploitation.

With these attitudes within them and surrounding them, it is exceptionally difficult for Zimbabwean women to become entrepreneurs; they will not do so unless there are challenges to culture. They will continue to regard themselves as secondary earners who do not have the responsibility of being breadwinners. They will remain trapped in small-scale, low-investment businesses, which cannot lead to 'liberating economic empowerment' that provides independence from men.

It is noticeable that men do not seem to be constrained in the same way from taking up work that is conventionally seen as women's. I have encountered male receptionists in the offices of multilateral agencies. Employers offer men doing such jobs opportunities to progress within the organisation and earn high salaries. Clearly, there is a need to encourage organisations to formulate gender policies, and to promote the practice of employing women in jobs that have been seen as men's, as well as employing men in jobs conventionally associated with women.

Structural barriers

Current restrictions to women's entrepreneurship lies in the differences in women's and men's involvement in business. The occupations women take up are defined by their skills, the resources they have available (including time, and their ability to travel, which are restricted by their caring role for the family), their role in the family, and cultural expectations.

Lack of marketable skills

Even when it appears that women are breaking out of 'traditional' roles by producing for cash, the nature of their involvement in serious entrepreneurship is determined by gender norms. Women may run small-scale businesses. They commonly sell commodities made in or near the home, out of materials that are home-grown. Alternatively, they may use the skills they have been taught as children, in their caring role — mainly sewing, cooking, and doing crochet. However, the products and services have a lower market value and are less in demand than carpentry, tin-smithing and manufacturing of heavy equipment: all done by men.

Zimbabwean women's businesses tend to be small, and most are not supported by the legal system, which is based on male standards and language. Many women trade in agricultural produce including vegetables, fruits, small animals, birds and pigs. Others engage in production of crafts, while quite a number buy and sell commodities that are available in their areas or they travel to get items for re-sale.

Time and ability to travel

Men are often much more enterprising in their choice of what to sell, due to a mixture of time resources and opportunity, and the fact that cultural beliefs allow them more scope than women have. For example, men are freer to go out and find products to sell that originate far from home. Women have to care for families, and most find it much harder than men to make arrangements to be away from home. It is common to hear comments such as: 'What is a woman doing at the market at this time of the day? She should be with her children at home, serving her husband.' Men maintain that women have a role at home and should not be engaging in vigorous business activities, which involve mingling with men in those sectors social constructed as male. There is also a popular prejudice against women travelling; people say 'vanozohura' or 'vanobatwa kwiyo' ('they will become prostitutes', 'they will not be able to protect themselves').

Most often, these reasons can be used to men's economic advantage. In the commercial farm workers sector, farm owners often choose female candidates for the position of farm health worker. An evaluation of farm workers' experiences in Maconi District showed that when the farm owners subsequently learnt that these workers would have to go away from the farm village for training (on courses that, incidentally, offered participants an attendance allowance), they selected men instead; the justification given was that women could not cope with the travelling (SNV NECAIZ 1998).

In some cases, women do succeed in extending their businesses in scale and across wider areas. Some become migrants: Zimbabwean women cross national borders into Botswana, South Africa, or travel as far as Namibia and Tanzania, to trade crafts and buy wares to sell back at home. While most women who venture far are single mothers or divorced women, obliged to support themselves, there is no reason why women cannot be assertive enough to travel and carry out their business. Risk-taking is a quality needed in entrepreneurship.

Land and assets

Gendered patterns of ownership and control of assets impact on women's ability to build businesses in many contexts, including my own. Women do not have collateral to engage in large-scale business activities that could generate real wealth, such as ranch-farming or large-scale manufacturing.

Under customary law in Zimbabwe, women do not own land or inherit land (Chenaux-Repond 1993). Land is owned and inherited by males. The woman's role is to farm for their fathers and later for their husbands, and finally for their sons, on land that they do not own. The harvested product is not theirs either, but men's property. For example, in a cotton farming rural area in Gokwe in the Midlands province, the number of female suicides has been reported in the national and regional press as rising after every cotton marketing season (*The Mail and Guardian*, 18 August 1998). Women commit suicide because their husbands collect the cheques from the Cotton Marketing Board, and the women never see the money. If they demand the money, they may be beaten or other acts of violence may be perpetrated against them. One woman was killed by her husband for planting seed in a manner different from that dictated by him (*Herald*, 20 January 1998). Women are unpaid and unacknowledged workers for their male relatives, and their labour is accrued to the men's assets.

Education

The importance of literacy and education for women in business is impossible to overemphasise. Illiteracy limits women to working at the lowest level of the informal sector. Development interventions need to focus on education as a pre-requisite to entrepreneurship.

Position as primary family providers

Women's responsibilities as family carers have direct implications for their business strategies. Women farmers who grow food for their families and communities may adopt very different strategies in their businesses from men. If a woman is the primary carer, profit can rarely be considered as 'surplus' to be invested in the business itself. Many women will use it to meet immediate family needs, such as school fees, or to buy basic necessities such as salt, oil and clothes for the family.

Current policy approaches to women entrepreneurs

As stated at the start of this article, much work has been done to date by development workers to enable entrepreneurs in rural areas of Zimbabwe to improve their skills. Most approaches emphasise vocational skills training, augmented by training in business skills and marketing. I find that women say the standard training materials are useful. Typically, they include material on choosing what product to produce and/or sell; selecting a location for the business; distribution and promotion; evaluating the product relevance to the customers; fixing a price for the goods or service; ensuring a good distribution of selling points; expanding the business; solving specific marketing problems; and developing marketing plans for given periods. Entrepreneurial training is accompanied by training in simple financial and project record-keeping. Finally, depending on the nature of the business, other specific skills training is usually offered. From my observation, businesses where such training is necessary include dressmaking, soap-making, crocheting, animal husbandry, and crop production. Women's organisations have tended to focus on the production of products that are associated with women and domesticity.

Even if the organisation is aware that this agenda may limit women, it may struggle to suggest training in non-traditional occupations since many organisations now ask women themselves to state their views and express their felt needs. In the absence of encouragement and awareness-raising about possible alternatives, it is natural that women will focus on familiar activities that are related to their existing roles.

What is missing from the current approaches?

In contrast, training needs identified through participatory approaches should focus on education, solving problems, and providing information. The problem with conventional approaches to entrepreneurship is that they do not focus on the need to challenge beliefs about women, men, money and power, or on making efforts to change the mind-sets of women and of society generally. The training itself usually takes place in a context in which women are given permission by their husbands (or mothers-in law if the husband is away at work) to attend workshops. Very little emphasis is placed on what aspects of human behaviour are required in the harsh male world of business and politics, and how this behaviour is constructed to disadvantage women. Women struggle to liberate themselves from the constraints culture places on them to exhibit qualities that do not seem to be in line with those required of entrepreneurs.

For example, at Project Making Sense workshops in Lupane, Matebeleand North, rural women I talked to complained that they could not be assertive with men because their culture did not allow it. Stories of women who have been conned by men in their micro-enterprises are numerous. I was told about a woman who bought ten bags of fish in Mangochi, in the southern region of Malawi, to sell in her village in Mulanje, and was helped by a young man to load them onto the bus to take home. At some point, the fish were stolen, but until she reached her destination the woman believed reassurances from the male bus conductor that her bags were safe. I believe, with my informant, that this woman lost all her fish because she was too trusting. That was the end of her enterprise. If this woman had been assertive, she would have checked at every stage that the fish was still on top of the bus.[1]

Existing approaches also fail to discuss and transfer the behavioural skills that make an individual an entrepreneur. For gender and development workers, the key questions here are 'can being an entrepreneur be compatible with the cultural values society associates with women?' and 'is being trusting incompatible with business'? When women get into business, our own internal programmes that we use to judge what is right and wrong, acceptable and unacceptable, often tell us that to behave like a man commonly behaves is inherently wrong. It does not feel right to do 'male' things and we may shy away from this challenge to gender roles, instead of deciding on the best course and forging on with business.

In fact, it should be possible to be an entrepreneur while still valuing the commitments to justice and fairness that are associated with women by communities in Zimbabwe. It is not only important to distinguish between what is seen as 'male' and 'female' behaviour, and to understand how behaviour is valued according to gender norms, but to see which behaviours (which may be associated with men or with women) are actually detrimental to society.

Conclusions

In southern Africa, as in other parts of the world, poverty is suffered more acutely by women and children than by men, since they are marginalised from decision-making and resources in all parts of society. Economic independence has, together with education, been identified as key to the emancipation of women and to national development. However, women entrepreneurs lack experience of leadership and command, due to women's generally low level of experience of leadership at community level. Development programmes focusing on women entrepreneurs in Zimbabwe have mainly concentrated on the practicalities of skills needed for production and marketing, rather than recognising that entre-preneurship is a foreign concept for most women. In addition, women need personal empowerment skills: assertiveness; skills in negotiating and balancing the tasks that women and men do in the family; time - management skills; and self-awareness. Programmes also need to focus on education for men so that they develop awareness of the effects of their behaviour on women, and a desire to change this.

Addressing constraints to entrepreneurship

While participatory methodologies, capacity building and strengthening of women have been the focus of development work in the last decade of the twentieth century, these concepts do not touch on the core of cultural patriarchal values that need to be reversed in order for women to gain economic independence. Effective entrepreneurship needs to be stimulated through the design and implementation of development activities that assist women to consider the aspects of their lives and culture that make it difficult for them to become entrepreneurs. A key strategy here is to put themselves in situations where the values they have learnt can be examined and questioned vigorously by others. The need for women to look at their values through the eyes of others and learn from them — especially those who have done well in business — is an important feature for programmes for women in the future. Values that are ethical but also effective need to be communicated with other would-be women entrepreneurs. To do all this, women need to cross cultural barriers that state that openness is dangerous in itself. For example, there is a saying in the Manyika dialect of Shona, *'mhere ngeineyi?'* (why the noise?), which is used when someone shares an idea openly. This encourages people to keep their views and ideas to themselves.

The need for macroeconomic policy change

Policies promoting women's role in economic production need to be formulated in the understanding of what women actually do, what they are capable of, and how they see themselves in their social setting. Only then can they enable women to realise their potential. Often women do not

act, not because they do not have the information or knowledge, but because there are macroeconomic factors that inhibit them. As mentioned above, women come for village-level entrepreneurial training because they are left in the village while men migrate for paid employment or to find more lucrative informal work in towns and cities. National-level policies should understand that this is because women undertake most of the reproductive work, and recognise the worth of this work, as well as the constraints that it puts on women's role in production. In no way should policy be formulated on the basis that women's work is ancillary to men's. Women are equal players in the economy at all levels.

Colletah Chitsike is a development consultant and trainer in rural development, organisational change and gender issues. She has an MA in Adult Education from the University of Zimbabwe. Her passions are gender and participatory approaches to development.

Note

1 Testimony collected during a workshop on Community Participation in Mulanje, Oxfam-funded project, Malawi 1991.

References

Chenaux-Repond, M (1993) 'Gender-biased land use rights in model: A resettlement schemes of Mashonaland', unpublished report.

ILO (1997) 'Second start your business impact evaluation report: Uganda, Zambia and Zimbabwe', unpublished.

Project Making Sense (1997) 'Use of multimedia to make sense of entrepreneurship', DFID/ActionAid/Radio for Development, unpublished report.

SNV NECAIZ (1998) 'An evaluation of farm workers, Makoni District, Zimbabwe', unpublished evaluation.

'Queering' development:
Exploring the links between same-sex sexualities, gender, and development

Susie Jolly

This article argues that gender and development policy and practice would be enhanced by embracing the challenges to conventional definitions of sex and gender that 'queer theory' poses. The author draws on insights from cultural studies, and discusses the experience of lesbian and gay activists from China as well as Europe and Africa.

In 1998, I facilitated a number of gender-awareness workshops in Beijing, run for Women's Federation officials from rural areas. The sessions began with everyone shouting out words associated with 'woman' and 'man'. Then we would discuss which words are applied exclusively to one sex. The usual conclusion we reached was that 'pretty', 'handsome', 'brave', or 'tender' could describe either women or men, but that 'beard', 'uterus', 'menstruation', or 'pregnancy' can apply only to one sex. At the end of the exercise, I would then reveal to them that they had discovered the distinction between sex and gender. Both these terms have recently been translated into Chinese as *shehui xingbie* ('social sex difference') and *shengli xingbie* ('biological sex difference').

During these exercises, I would think about the bar I knew in central Beijing which was popular with lesbians and gay men. The bar was always crowded with Chinese men — and sometimes a few women — playing games about gender identity with a consciousness that was different from the 'awareness' we were trying to promote through our gender training. In the bar, I had heard questions such as 'Of the two of you, who's the man, who's the woman?' and 'Are you a top or a bottom?'. Some boys referred to each other as 'sisters'. While these questions do not imply that gay men and lesbians are completely unrestricted as to which gender roles and identity we can assume, they do imply more flexibility in thinking. They implicitly recognise that it is not the body you are born with that dictates whether you have a gender identity as a 'boy' or a 'girl'; rather, it what you choose to do with it.

I wonder how these understandings of the complex relationship between one's body and one's gender identity might be brought into our gender training. It would not have been politically acceptable to hold an open meeting between rural Chinese government officials and cosmopolitan 'gay boys' from Beijing, and in any case, the clash of such different cultures might have rendered the exercise counter-productive. However, there must be ways to start such communication, which could well prove worthwhile.

During the past year, it seems that there has been greater interaction between lesbian, bisexual, and gay activists and individuals working on 'women's issues' in China. For example, Kim Wu, a lesbian activist, gave a presentation to academics at a national conference on feminism in Beijing (interview 1999). This interaction has started me thinking about the connections between same-sex sexualities and gender and development (henceforth abbreviated as GAD). I am interested in the following questions:

- Do theoretical approaches to same-sex sexualities have something to offer development theory and policy?

- Should GAD be concerned with questions of sexuality, including same-sex sexualities?

- Can same-sex sexualities be a focus for gender and development policy and practice, without replaying familiar North-South power dynamics which impose Western influences on yet another arena?

My ideas are informed by two academic disciplines, which I believe have much to offer each other. One is development studies, firmly located in the social sciences. The other is queer theory (a body of theories addressing same-sex sexualities, originating in lesbian studies, gay studies, and other forms of cultural studies, which I discuss later in this article). The article focuses on examples from China, where I spent six years of my life. Much of this time I lived in Beijing, working on poverty alleviation, and co-operating with local lesbian and gay activists in my spare time.

What can a focus on same-sex sexualities offer to GAD concepts?

During the last 15 years of the twentieth century, development policy and practice has shifted from women in development (WID) approaches to GAD approaches, denoting a change from a relatively narrow focus on women's disadvantages in male-dominated society, to a more politicised emphasis on power relations between women and men (Razavi and Miller 1995).

Linking the sexual and the material

Freedom to determine one's sexual behaviour is closely connected to economic and political freedoms. Feminists have long argued that constraints on women in sexual and economic realms are interconnected, hence the slogan 'the personal is political'. In particular, the marital relationship has physical, sexual, social, economic, and legal dimensions. 'The desire to control women's reproductive functioning and to maintain control over their sexuality has been a major impetus behind various restrictions on women's public role, ranging from seclusion and veiling to more subtle pressures and disincentives ... There are sexual and nonsexual reasons for women's subordinate status, and... these reasons interact and reinforce one another in many different ways ... [S]exual desire itself is shaped by structures of power and subordination; I don't think that the distinction between the "sexual" and "nonsexual" is, or should be, a sharp one' (Nussbaum 1999, 17).

Gender norms concerned with sexuality shape both women's and men's lives, including rules determining how, and with whom, women and men should engage sexually. For example, there are rules on whether sex should happen only within marriage; how many wives or husbands we should marry; and whether or not we should sleep only with people of the opposite sex. These norms are all-pervasive, and not only determine the sexual aspect of our lives, but also shape our access to economic resources, and our ability to participate in social and political activities. For women, failure to marry may restrict access to vital resources such as land or housing, while at the same time, marriage at its worst may make women vulnerable to marital rape and violence.

80

GAD policy-makers and practitioners have argued that if women are to gain greater choice over their sexual relationships, they need sufficient economic and social bargaining power to enable them to exercise their choices, since those who stray from the norms of female sexuality in many societies — including heterosexuality and chastity before marriage as well as fidelity and constant sexual availability within it — face social sanctions which affect their livelihoods and well-being. For example, a woman who lives in an Islamic society where purdah (female seclusion) is practised may decide to violate purdah in order to participate in income-generating work. By doing this, she is simultaneously threatening the economic control and the sexual control of men over her life. GAD's analysis of the connections between the control of sexuality and economic and political power can be extended to examine the unjust treatment meted out not only to women as a sex, but to all who deviate from prescribed gender roles.

Feminists and gay activists as 'other'

Those who challenge gender norms sexually or otherwise are often stereotyped as a dangerous 'other'. Some Third World commentators have gone further, responding to feminist writings by denouncing such ideas as Western impositions on traditional cultures. 'Western feminism' has been labelled 'cultural imperialism' by politicians in Zimbabwe (Seidman 1984, 432). Such accusations, common in many countries, can create a difficult climate for Southerners who advocate gender equality. They are always vulnerable to the charge of putting 'Western' values before 'tradition' and patriotism. In Taiwan for example, Women's Studies academics are under pressure to demonstrate their difference from 'Western feminism', and to prove that they are 'Chinese enough' (Ding and Liu 1999, 140). Both feminism and the movement for lesbian and gay liberation have been charged in this way.

'The widespread stereotyping of both feminists and gays and lesbians as underminers of traditional social order gives us one strong reason to study the two sets of issues together, asking what definitions of maleness and femaleness underlie both the fear of feminism and the opposition to equal civil rights for lesbians and gay men. Thus, legal theorists have recently argued that resistance to full equality for gays is a form of sex discrimination in the sense that it is a device for maintaining fixed divisions between the male and the female, which, in turn, are traditionally linked with a hierarchical placement of male over female.' (Nussbaum 1999, 15)

Human rights perspectives

Since the start of the HIV/AIDS epidemic, it has become clear that sexual activity is a life-and-death issue for women and men throughout the world — regardless of their sexual orientation. However, sexual orientation itself is also a matter of life and death for the many women and men in same-sex relationships who face homophobic violence, in their homes and in the public sphere.

Homophobic violence is a common problem worldwide. In 1999 a US soldier, Barry Winchell, was beaten to death by another soldier in a killing motivated by homophobia ('Army Death Spurs Criticism of Policy', Associated Press, Yahoo News, 10 December 1999). Transvestites have been murdered in Mexico, gay men imprisoned under sodomy laws in Romania, and lesbians and gay men executed in Iran (Rosenbloom 1996). Suicides among lesbians have been reported in North and South: one case is that of Gita Darji and Kishori Shah in India, who killed themselves together rather than allow their relationship to be broken up by their families (ibid.). A Zimbabwean woman reported being raped with her family's knowledge and consent so that she would get pregnant, marry, and cease to have relationships with women: '[My girlfriend and I] are always on the run because my parents are against what I am. When they found out that I was a lesbian, they tried to force me to find a boyfriend … in the end they forced an old man on me. They locked me in a room and brought him every day to rape me, so I would fall pregnant and be forced to marry him' (ibid., 234). This woman had no recourse to help from the authorities in a country where the President, Robert Mugabe, has stated publicly of homosexuals 'I don't believe they should have any rights at all' (Phillips 1999, 3).

Human rights activists have pointed out that '[w]omen's rights and lesbian rights are linked in substantive ways. Both issues challenge how human rights distinctions between the private and public and reluctance to address female sexuality have perpetuated violations of women and kept them invisible. Further, the defense of lesbian rights is integral to the defense of all women's right to determine their own sexuality, to work at the jobs they prefer, and to live as they choose with women, men, children or alone.' (Charlotte Bunch, in Rosenbloom 1996, vi). As the examples given here demonstrate, protection from homophobic violence is a basic — and urgent — need.

GAD's reluctance to engage with same-sex sexualities

Development policy and practice have tended to avoid discussions of sexuality, beyond debates on population and, more recently, HIV and AIDS. It has been argued that the exclusion of sexuality from development agendas suggests the problematic assumption that while in the North people need sex and love, in the South they just need to eat (Wieringa 1998). In fact, lack of freedom to express sexuality can threaten survival, the most basic of human needs.

In addition to the focus on narrow interpretations of basic needs, there are several other possible reasons for GAD's reluctance to address questions of sexuality. In this section, I will look at three.

'What right do we have to intervene in local culture?'

This question is the 'flip-side' of the objections raised by commentators from developing countries who accuse feminists and gay activists of Western domination. It is often asked by Western development practitioners in the context of GAD programmes which directly address relations between individual women and individual men, including sexual concerns. Interfering in 'culture' appears to be much less of a concern for most in interventions dealing with issues such as poverty alleviation, implying that a double standard is in operation: 'Why is it that challenging gender inequalities is seen as tampering with traditions or culture, and thus taboo, while challenging inequalities in terms of wealth and class is not?' (Metha cited in Smyth 1999). The question of the right of outsiders to intervene should be asked of all projects, economic or otherwise.

One possible answer is that 'women belong to cultures. But they do not choose to be born into any particular culture, and they do not really choose to endorse its norms as good for themselves, unless they do so in possession of further options and opportunities—including the opportunity to form communities of affiliation and empowerment with other women' (Nussbaum 1999, 54). Different groups and individuals have different stakes in, and feelings of belonging to, the cultures in which they live. Development interventions can play a part in raising women's awareness of the 'further options and affiliations' which may exist. They may do the same for sexual minorities. Those who feel constrained by certain aspects of their culture could be offered the choice whether to aim for an alternative, or to consciously validate 'their' culture.

However, while the introduction of an alternative option by outside forces can be liberating, new options rarely appear as neutral choices. This is particularly evident in the economic arena, where the worldwide spread of free-market economics can hardly be interpreted as having been a free choice by national governments. 'Globalisation' of economic systems has been accompanied by cultural influences which sweep people along, often appearing to be the only profitable or viable option. This process has challenged, and often changed, understandings of gender and sexuality throughout the world.

'Homosexuality comes from the West'

Homosexuality is often stereotyped as a Western phenomenon; for example, President Mugabe of Zimbabwe has attacked homosexuality as 'non-traditional' and 'un-African', in spite of numerous historical records and contemporary voices from the South which contest his view, including that of the organisation Gays and Lesbians of Zimbabwe (*Queer Africa Digest*, 10 January 2000).

At the 1985 Decade World Conference on Women in Nairobi, Third World lesbians released the following press statement: 'If it seems that lesbianism is confined to white western women, it is often because third world lesbians and lesbians of colour come up against more obstacles to our visibility — but this silence has to be seen as one more aspect of women's sexual repression and not as a conclusion that lesbianism doesn't concern us ... The struggle for lesbian rights is indispensable to any struggle for basic human rights. It's part of the struggle for all women for control over our own lives' (cited in Rosenbloom 1996, v).

'Let's not risk bringing the clumsy "development machine" into more intimate areas of people's lives'

'Post-development' theorists have argued that in spite of the rhetoric of good intentions, development has largely functioned as a means to continue colonial control in the South (Rahnema et al. 1997). Whether or not one accepts this view, many would agree that the legacy of the development industry is at best mixed. Do we really want to encourage the clumsy 'development machine' into even more intimate areas of people's lives? Do we trust it to approach sexualities with any level of awareness and sensitivity? I look at some Chinese views concerning these questions in the following section.

Tongzhi, globalisation, and gay identities

In the context of China, homosexual behaviour and love are *not* seen as Western; however, particular gay identities *are*. In the next sections, I will discuss the way in which these identities are coming into context with *tongzhi* (literally, 'common will'). This is the Chinese word for 'comrade' which many lesbian, bisexual, and gay people in mainland China, Hong Kong, and Taiwan now use to refer to themselves. How have these identities appeared in China? Are they appropriate to Chinese contexts, and are they being imposed, or simply offered as an option? I will also examine the role of non-Chinese activists like myself in this process.

Discussions of Chinese gay identities

A press release for the 1998 Chinese *Tongzhi* Conference in Hong Kong declared: 'The lesbi-gay movement in many Western societies is largely built upon the notion of individualism, confrontational politics, and the discourse of individual rights. Certain characteristics of confrontational politics, such as coming out and mass protests and parades, may not be the best way of achieving *tongzhi* liberation in the family-centered, community-oriented Chinese societies which stress the importance of social harmony. In formulating the *tongzhi* movement strategy, we should take the specific socio-economic and cultural environment of each society into consideration' (*International News* No.201, 1998).

Zhou Huashan, a writer from Hong Kong, argues along similar lines that a more harmonious family-based approach will be an effective strategy for Chinese *tongzhi*. He also makes the case that China has a tradition of same-sex love (particularly in the case of men), which did not encounter such violent hostility as in the West, and points out that homophobia in China originated in colonial Christian influences in the nineteenth century. In contrast, Wu, an activist in Beijing, contests Zhou Huashan's position: 'If you insist on starting from the Chinese homosexual tradition ... well, married men historically could have one, two, three boyfriends, but this was by sacrificing the wife. This is where I disagree with Zhou Huashan's claim that in China we're always harmonious' (interview, Brighton, 1999).

Wu argues that international experience may be more relevant than Chinese 'tradition' to Beijing *tongzhi* today. She also believes that it is possible to 'pick and mix' aspects of foreign influence, rather than swallow it whole: 'If I look at what's happening [in the les-bi-gay movement] in the Philippines, England, Holland, I will consider what are they like because of the historical, cultural, and social situation. I'll ask a lot of questions, then I'll think, what would it be like if we tried that in China? ... Seeing a lot of different things is very important. Even if the information all came from the West, the West is big and varied. So we have to see how individuals deal with this.' (ibid.)

Engaging with international organisations and donors

Such debates are a live issue, as information, funding, and support from international organisations and individuals start to trickle into the *tongzhi* scene in Chinese cities. On a tiny scale, 'development assistance' to *tongzhi* has begun. Ming, another Beijing organiser, notes that such support was instrumental to the establishment of the Beijing Sisters, a lesbian group in Beijing: 'To start with, our activities mostly took place in foreigners' homes, because foreigners are not afraid of coming out: they have the material conditions to provide a place for activities, and also experience of organising. So that's how women *tongzhi* activities started. But our activities were criticised by some for being centred around foreigners, imperialist-led, and so on. We are very happy to be criticised like this, because we do indeed need our own women *tongzhi* organisations and leadership, but we also welcome help and support from foreign imperialists with experience and enthusiasm. Without the help of these "foreign imperialists", sooner or later we would have established our own organisation, but because of their support, we emerged a few years earlier than we might have done otherwise. Although I don't really agree with excluding imperialists, I still think this is worth raising as an issue.' (Ming 1999, 5). Ming also notes the dangers of support from 'outsiders', but they are Chinese heterosexual 'experts' who research *tongzhi*, rather than foreign lesbian women (although one such 'heterosexual expert' appeared one day with a girlfriend in place of her husband, illustrating the fluidity of such categories).

Ming describes the Beijing Sisters' co-operation with *tongzhi* men as involving certain tensions, but says 'if even foreign imperialists can join us, then we can't exclude boys ... Race and the North-South divide are only a part of what unites and divides us. The foreigner-Chinese relation is only one of many aspects of women *tongzhi* co-operation with "outsiders". I do not imagine that "the global sisterhood" or queer comradeship can erase North-South power differences.' Nevertheless, alliances cross all kinds of fault-lines, and divisions occur in all kinds of alliances. The interaction is complex, and 'alien' values — whether foreign, male, heterosexual, or 'expert' — are not necessarily simply and easily imposed.

Wu remains optimistic regarding such impositions, and the capacity of *tongzhi* to select which, if any, elements of Western queer culture to accept. She locates the dangers of globalisation not here, but in areas where more powerful forces are at play: 'The scariest thing about globalisation is those who've studied in the West for many years who come back [to China] to work for multinational companies. They've completely accepted Western things, and know how to promote these things effectively in China' (interview, Brighton, 1999). She suggests the best course of action is to provide as much information as possible, so that 'we can choose whether to adopt, and how to apply,' outside influences. She advises, 'You should worry less about influencing us with your concepts, and think more about how to support us' (ibid.).

I cite this discussion not in the hope of reaching any conclusions about how development, queer or otherwise, should deal with North-South power imbalances and persistent colonial dynamics. I wish only to point out that these issues are being actively debated in some Southern contexts, and that such voices should be listened to in any decision processes on if or how to 'queer' development.

Does 'queer theory' have something to offer development?

In the late 1980s, the term 'queer' (originally an insult for marginalised sexualities and other 'deviants') was reclaimed and invested with new meanings by activists in the USA. Formerly, with the use of the word 'homosexual', we had been defined in relation to heterosexuality. The labels 'lesbian' and 'gay' also marked us with supposedly bounded, static identities which could be clearly differentiated from 'straight'. The use of the word 'queer' constituted a rejection of the binary distinction between homo- and heterosexual, and allowed us to conceptualise our sexualities as non-essential and transitional. 'Queer' was to be a new approach to sexuality, open to all those who are oppressed by these binary distinctions and the gender norms which accompany them, whether they are lesbian, gay, straight, bisexual, transgender, transsexual, celibate, undecided, or hermaphrodite. The idea of queer was taken up by academics, particularly in the USA and Britain, whose work has become known as 'queer theory'.

Queer theory on sex and gender

Much GAD work (for example, the gender awareness course I taught in Beijing) is still based on the dichotomy between biological sex and social gender. However, queer theorists such as Judith Butler have pointed out that there is no 'pure' biological body on to which social ideas of gender are inscribed. Rather, our bodies and our social identities are interactive. Henrietta Moore describes the body as an 'interface' or 'threshold' between the material and symbolic, the biological and cultural (Moore 1994). Our experiences have implications for the appearance, condition, and performance of our bodies. For example, women may have hysterectomies, bear children or not, remove or grow body or facial hair. Both men and women may or may not exercise until they are muscular, or suffer from war or sports injuries.

Judith Butler argues that bodies are understood by society through our ideas about sex and gender. People are categorised as men or women according to their potential capacity for pregnancy, or their type of sexual organs, but she sees this not as a simple description of reality, but rather as the outcome of a decision on the part of society to stress the importance of certain aspects of our bodies, rather than others, and the importance of particular differences between bodies. Even the ability to become pregnant and bear children, which is viewed by most people as the determining factor defining women, is questioned: '...female infants and children cannot be impregnated, there are women of all ages who cannot be impregnated,' (Butler 1994, 34). In fact, there may be as great a variation between a group of bodies of one sex, as between bodies of different sexes.

Judith Butler stresses that it is those in power who decide which biological differences between people will put them in particular categories. Similarities between bodies of one 'biological' sex are exaggerated, and differences between bodies of different sexes are played down. Those who do not fit these two categories are effectively made to disappear, either by being shamed into secrecy, or by physical intervention, such as operations on hermaphrodites at birth (Valentine et al. 1997). Thus, although the categories of sex *appear* natural and absolute, they are 'cleaned up' by active human intervention.

Butler goes on to ask: 'Why are we defined by our reproductive capacities? This is 'an imposition of a norm, not a neutral description of biological constraints... If you are in your late twenties or your early thirties and you can't get pregnant for biological reasons, or maybe you don't want to, for social reasons — whatever it is — you are struggling with a norm that is regulating your sex.' (ibid., 34)

If, as Butler argues, we are classified as men or women due to the way society sees our bodies and wants us to use them, rather than because of the nature of our bodies themselves, then the category of biological sex, as well as gender, can be challenged. And if biological sex loses its essential meaning, then same-sex and different-sex desire also cease to be absolutely distinct, fixed categories, and — like sex and gender — are revealed to be socially and politically constructed. Instead of being unchangeable, our sex and our sexuality, like our gender identity, depends on how we choose to behave moment by moment.

Putting queer into practice in development

Where does this challenge to the idea of biological sex as universal and unchanging leave GAD? One option is to continue using GAD's present categorisations of sex and gender — not because we believe they necessarily capture objective truth in the real world, but because they are practical to work with. However, for social policy-makers to deliberately ignore new research on gender issues does not seem a promising strategy. Alternatively, GAD could adopt a second strategy of challenging the binary distinctions between sex and gender as we find them in our gender training materials, and exploring new, queer ways of understanding sex and gender, for example using Theatre for Development.

Judith Butler's ideas and discussions of potential ways forward, are already filtering through into GAD literature (Kandiyoti 1998; Wieringa 1998). These thoughts challenge GAD policy and practice to live up to their promise to focus on gender relations, not simply on women as a category. Many GAD programmes still work only with women. The focus could be shifted to those marginalised by gender norms, or those who lack power, and away from the simple distinction between women and men. (Of course, we have to be practical; identifying individuals with less power in a specific context would be much more complicated than selecting members from the known categories of women or men. I myself have taken part in women-only feminist groups, and argued for micro-credit loans in a poverty alleviation project to be targeted exclusively at women. However, such criteria can often involve compromises made at a hidden cost.)

How development practice would be queered is a big question that is as yet unexplored. However, some implications are already visible. There is both a need to target queers specifically, and to mainstream 'queer' into social policy and GAD. In the following, I outline ways of going about this.

Targeting queer groups for support

Donor support to Southern queer communities, like any other international development assistance, can involve either unacceptable, clumsy, and inappropriate imposition of alien values, or an emphasis on mutual learning, capacity-building, and transferring ideas on 'best practice'. Development assistance of the latter kind to queer groups in Southern countries is already starting — albeit on a small scale — via international funding and support to activities in countries including China, Zimbabwe, and South Africa (see International Lesbian and Gay Association, http://www.ilga.org). Queer initiatives do have some advantages over more traditional development: their small scale, unofficial nature, and activist element may mean they stand more hope of being reclaimed and controlled by local people.

Adapting perceptions of the community, household, and family

Many development interventions have the household as a primary focus, due to a growing awareness in both economics and sociology that the household is far from a homogeneous unit, and that resources within the family are not distributed equally, particularly along gender and age lines (Kabeer 1994). However, there is little or no research into the way in which people who have minority sexual identities figure in relation to their communities, households, or families.

In some contexts, where there is a visible minority of these individuals, 'alternative' family or community groups have been set up. However, most people remain within conventional family set-ups. While some do develop sexual relationships with members of the same sex (perhaps with a degree of secrecy), others do not, denying who they are at some emotional cost.

Notions of the household model need to be adjusted in order to render visible the way in which queer members of the household are integrated, both socially and economically, and to understand the decisions they take to conform, or resist conformity, to norms of marriage, parenthood, and the gender division of labour. Approaches developed by queer researchers and activists to understand same-sex relationships within the household could be fruitfully adapted to look at *heterosexual* situations: 'Same-sex households provide an avenue to expand our understanding of gender itself [for example, where gender-stereotypical behaviour patterns occur between people of the same sex] and the nature of the relationship between gender and the sexual division of labour' (Giddings 1998, 97).

Integrating queer into health, education, and youth work

Development interventions in the health and education sectors — particularly those working with young people — also need to integrate awareness of specific issues affecting people who have same-sex sex. Most obviously, much is at stake for men who have sex with men, and for their wives or female partners. Just as men can put their female partners at risk by having unsafe sex with other women, some also do so by having unsafe sex with other men. Safer sex and AIDS-related education programmes can benefit from the experience of gay communities. However, while the promotion of safer sex is of course a major task, so is the prevention of physical, especially sexual, violence against sexual minorities, and protection of their mental health in the face of such pressures.

Institutionalising queer

If GAD workers do try to move the field onwards by taking on some of the insights offered by queer theory, they need to be fully aware of the need to queer development institutions themselves. This would include acknowledging the existence of same-sex partnerships among their own staff, extending the rights and benefits offered to heterosexual couples (for example, to health care) to same-sex partners of staff, and integrating queer awareness into staff training (for example, through diversity training).

Concluding thoughts

There may be many more implications of queer experience for feminist action and GAD policy and practice. Michael Warner argues that 'queer theory is opening up in the way that feminism did, when feminists began treating gender more and more as a primary category for understanding problems that did not initially look gender-specific ... we do not know yet what it would be like to make sexuality a primary category for social theory' (Warner 1993, xv). In my view, queer experience and theory has much to offer GAD. Likewise, development assistance could provide vital support to Southern women and men who face marginalisation and oppression as a consequence of their refusal to conform to conventional sexual norms. As I found in my work in China, queer activists, feminists, and GAD workers can form alliances with the shared goal of challenging prescribed roles based on static, 'natural', and universal notions of sex and/or gender. Ideally, queer and GAD activists and thinkers can engage in a process of mutual support and learning, taking on the common obstacles posed by oppressive gender norms.

Susie Jolly is a queer feminist activist and development practitioner. She is currently studying at the Institute of Development Studies, University of Sussex, Brighton BN1 9RE, UK. E-mail: idpn8@ids.ac.uk

References

Butler, J (1990) *Gender Trouble*, Routledge, London.

Butler, J (1994) 'Gender as performance: An interview with Judith Butler', *Radical Philosophy*, Summer.

Naifei Ding and Liu Jen-peng (1998) 'The penumbra asks the shadow: Reticent poetics and queer politics', *Gender Research*, 3:4 (written in Chinese, English translation available).

Giddings, L (1998) 'Political economy and the construction of gender: The example of housework within same-sex households', *Feminist Economics*, 4:2.

International Lesbian and Gay Association website: http://www.ilga.org

International News No.201 (March 1998) '200 at Chinese Tongzhi conference in Hong Kong', website: http://www.dakini .org/news/98/7.htm

Kabeer, N (1994) *Reversed Realities: Gender Hierarchies in Development Thought*, Verso, London.

Kandiyoti, D (1998) 'Gender, power and contestation: Rethinking bargaining with patriarchy' in Jackson, C and Pearson, R (eds) (1998) *Feminist Visions of Development*, Routledge, London.

Ming (1999) 'Beijing sisters and Tongzhi hotline', unpublished conference paper, 'Women Organising in China', Oxford, July 1999 (written in Chinese).

Moore, H (1994) *A Passion for Difference*, Polity Press, London.

Nussbaum, M (1999) *Sex and Social Justice*, Oxford University Press.

Phillipps, O (1999) 'Sexual Offences in Zimbabwe: Fetishisms of procreation, perversion and individual autonomy', unpublished PhD dissertation, Institute of Criminology, University of Cambridge.

Queer Africa Digest (10 January 2000), e-mail newsletter, 1:137.

Rahnema, M and Bawtree, V (eds) (1997) *The Post-Development Reader*, Zed Books, London.

Rosenbloom, R (ed) (1996) *Unspoken Rules: Sexual orientation and women's human rights*, Cassell, London.

Razave, S and Miller, C (1995) 'From WID to GAD: Conceptual shifts in the women and development discourse', occasional paper, UNRISD.

Seidman, GW (1984) 'Women in Zimbabwe: Post-Independence struggles', *Feminist Studies*, 10:3, Fall.

Smyth, I (1999) 'A rose by any other name: Feminism in development NGOs', in Porter, F, Smyth, I and Sweetman, C (eds) (1999) *Gender Works: Oxfam experience in policy and practice*, Oxfam, Oxford.

Valentine, D and Wilchins, RA (1997) 'One percent on the burn chart', *Social Text*, 52-53 Fall-Winter, 215-22.

Warner, M (ed) (1993) *Fear of a Queer Planet: Queer politics and social theory*, University of Minnesota Press, Minneapolis.

Wieringa, S (1998) 'Rethinking gender planning: A critical discussion of the use of the concept gender', ISS Working Paper Series, No. 279.

Wu, Kim (1999), unpublished interview by Susie Jolly (in Chinese).

Zhou, H (1997) *Post-colonial Tongzhi*, Hong Kong Tongzhi Research Institute Publishing House (written in Chinese).

Challenging *machismo*:

Promoting sexual and reproductive health with Nicaraguan men

Peter Sternberg

Health education work with men needs to be done from a gender perspective, which encourages men not only to take on responsibility for promoting health, but also to share that responsibility with women. This article presents the results of a participatory exploration of men's attitudes towards sexual and reproductive health issues in Nicaragua.

Men's participation in sexual health promotion is seen by many as a promising strategy (Drennon 1998). However, apart from a small number of recent interventions such as Stepping Stones, an HIV prevention programme based on gender relationships (Welbourn 1995), and Fathers Inc., a Jamaican peer-based approach to adolescent men's sexual health (Lize 1998), health promotion has been slow to take up the challenge.

In 1996, the Centro de Información y Servicios de Asesoría en Salud (CISAS), a prominent Nicaraguan health-promotion NGO, began working with groups of men, mainly in response to demands by women from some of the poor communities where it works. The women argued that it is all very well working with women and girls to promote sexual and reproductive health and empowerment, but if you really want things to change, you have to work with men too.

From its inception in 1983, CISAS has worked from a perspective of community empowerment, with a particular emphasis on empowering women. However, CISAS has recognised that many organisations' health-promotion agenda is conservative and male-oriented, generally viewing women as vehicles for reproduction or the transmission of illness, rather than as valued individuals (Wilton 1994). This stance not only ignores women's needs as individuals (Doyal 1991), but also ignores men as a group (Barker 1996). As a result, such approaches reiterate women's responsibility for health, especially for reproductive health, while ignoring the possibility that men could play a positive and proactive role alongside women in promoting their own health and the health of their families and communities (Wegner et al. 1998).

There is a stereotype of men as sexually voracious, careless, and irresponsible. Men who conform to this stereotype are unlikely to be much concerned about the possibilities of fathering an unplanned child or of contracting HIV or other sexually trans-mitted diseases. However, the stereotype is not borne out by reality. For example, citing his own research carried out in Puerto Rico in the 1950s, Stycos, the veteran health promoter and family planner, stresses that the men he interviewed were far from 'the sex-crazed males anxious to demonstrate their fertility' (Stycos 1996, 2) he had been led to expect. What he found instead was that expectations and norms of male and female behaviour made communication between men and women, especially on matters to do with sex and sexuality, very difficult. Stycos identified this lack of communication between the genders as an important aspect governing sexual behaviour, and concluded that there was a need to work with men in highlighting the benefits of family planning to them as individuals. It is only by establishing a men's agenda in reproductive health that things will change, a lesson, Stycos says, which has too often been ignored; it is a lesson which CISAS is taking seriously.

CISAS hoped, through this research, to provide men with a body of information that they could use to understand their behaviour, attitudes, and the context of these, in order to develop an awareness of the social and cultural norms defined by *machismo*, and the way these norms create a certain model of 'acceptable' male sexual behaviour, and a particular set of attitudes. Individual men needed to consider how similar their actual behaviour and attitudes are to the stereotypical model of masculinity with which they are presented, the model that in Nicaragua makes up the *machismo* system. Second, CISAS aimed to encourage men to consider the effect of their behaviour on themselves and on other people. It was hoped that, by helping men to think through these issues, it would be possible to change the power relationships which lead individual men to put themselves and others at risk.

The Nicaraguan context

Following the revolution in Nicaragua in 1979[1], one of the aims of the Sandinista government was to foster more stable and egalitarian families, and to enshrine equal rights for women within the constitution (Lancaster 1992). In this aim, as in so many others, the Sandinistas failed due to a combination of war, bad planning, and economic instability which culminated, in 1990, in their electoral defeat.

The two governments that followed have pursued neo-liberal monetarist policies, and adopted structural adjustment programmes set up by the World Bank (Vargas 1998). Over the past ten years, these policies have caused not only rising prices and stagnating wages, but also a rise in unemployment and a rapid expansion of the 'informal economy'. The gap between the 'haves' and the 'have nots' has widened dramatically: today, over 70 per cent of the population live below the poverty line (ibid.). Managua, once one of the safest cities in Latin America, has become a battle ground for rival gangs of young men; violent crime, robbery, prostitution, and sexual tourism are on the increase (CENIDH 1998). The country and the economy have also been afflicted by a series of natural disasters, culminating with Hurricane Mitch in 1998. Some 865,700 people were directly affected by the hurricane, losing their homes, their livelihoods or both (Alforja 1999).

One result of this instability has been the exponential growth of Nicaragua's civil society since 1990, a reaction to the gaps left through government inaction and lack of interest. CISAS and other Nicaraguan NGOs have been at the forefront of championing human rights, and have managed to keep gender power relations more or less on the policy agenda. Nicaraguan NGOs have had some notable successes, including the passing of a law that made intrafamilial violence a crime punishable by imprisonment, and the establishment of several pilot projects of a new police service staffed by officers specially trained to deal with crimes against women and children. Despite these initiatives, police reported that in 1998, crimes against women and children had increased by 17 per cent from their 1997 levels (INEC 1999).

Nicaraguan women continue to be under-represented in the public sphere and abused in their private lives (Montenegro

1997). Only 11 per cent of National Assembly legislators and 25 per cent of the Nicaraguan members of the Central American Parliament are women (CENIDH 1998). The official 1998 demographic and health survey, ENDESA-98, found that 29 per cent of Nicaraguan women have been physically or sexually abused by their male partners. Of these, over 46 per cent had been abused in the previous 12 months (INEC 1999). The Nicaraguan media is conservative in its representation of women (Montenegro 1997), a fact brought home to many Nicaraguans by their virtual silence on former Sandinista president Daniel Ortega's continuing refusal to recant his senatorial immunity in order to answer charges of sexual abuse brought by his stepdaughter in 1998.[2]

Health and sexuality in Nicaragua

Statistics about sexual and reproductive health in Nicaragua reveal that although almost all of the women (more than 95 per cent) who took part in the 1998 national demographic survey had heard of modern contraceptive methods, only 60 per cent of women of fertile age were users in 1998 (ibid.). Some 15 per cent of women consider their contraceptive needs unmet (ibid.). Although contraception is legally available, government policy emphasises the need for sexual morality and abstinence until marriage (GHCV 1997). Sex education in schools is taught within a framework of 'family values', which views sex as a necessary evil for perpetuating the species (ibid.). This may be one of the reasons why the Nicaraguan fertility rate is one of the highest in Latin America, at an average of 3.9 children per woman of fertile age (INEC 1999). It may also help to explain why by the age of 19, 46 per cent of women have been pregnant at some time (ibid.). In Nicaragua, abortion is illegal except for medical reasons, and even then, abortions can only be legally performed with the permission of three doctors, and the consent of the woman's partner or guardian. Unsurprisingly, there is a high rate of illegal abortions, many of which are performed under unsafe conditions (Pizarro 1996).

In 1998, the Ministry of Health recorded an incidence of 153 per 100,000 cases of sexually transmitted diseases (STDs). By September 1999, some 476 cases of HIV infection had been reported since 1987 in a population of 4.8m people. The Ministry of Health recognises that there is substantial under-reporting of STDs including HIV, and the actual figures are probably much higher (MINSA 1999). The organisation that co-ordinates HIV prevention initiatives for Central America argues that although reported numbers of infections are low, the population is at risk because of its young demographic profile, high fertility rate, and low or irregular usage of condoms (PASCA 1997).

Machismo and the Nicaraguan man

Almost without exception, studies of gender and sexuality in Nicaragua highlight one overarching aspect of the culture: *machismo*. There is no English word which adequately translates this term, but *machismo* could be described as a cult of the male; a heady mixture of paternalism, aggression, systematic subordination of women, fetishism of women's bodies, and idolisation of their reproductive and nurturing capacities, coupled with a rejection of homosexuality. The Central American psychologist, Martín Baró, characterises it as a strong tendency towards, and valuing of, genital activity (that is, penetration); a frequent tendency towards bodily aggression; a carefully cultivated devil-may-care attitude or indifference towards any activity which does not clearly reinforce masculinity; and *Guadalupismo*, a hypersensitivity towards the idealised notion of women as virgins or mothers (Baró 1988).

Machismo is not just present in the behaviour of individual men: it is manifested in political and social institutions and deeply ingrained in the culture (Monzón 1988). *Machismo* has been seen as a system of political organisation — 'a political economy of the body' (Lancaster 1992, 236) — in which the cult of the male is an important underpinning of the productive and reproductive economy. *Machismo* gives rise to powerful images that legitimate women's subordination and establish a value system which is concerned with regulating not so much relationships between men and women, but relationships between men, where women are conceived of as a form of currency.

A serious problem with using *machismo* to explain men's behaviour is that the cultural values which surround *machismo* are constantly being redefined. This state of flux seems to be an integral part of Nicaraguan society: as the political commentator and sociologist, Oscar Rene Vargas, points out: 'As a country, Nicaragua is eternally searching for an identity and oscillating, in an ambivalent way, between old and modern, tradition and fashion, native and foreign.' (Vargas 1999, 19; my translation). This oscillation belies any attempt to explain Nicaraguan culture, or the political and social system, in terms of single-word concepts like *machismo*, or for that matter 'neoliberal', 'conservative' and 'catholic'. Such labels cannot be used, either, to explain or predict men's behaviour. However, helping Nicaraguan men understand themselves, and the way in which *machismo* operates in their lives, might provide men with reasons to participate in actions aimed at altering the oppressive structures which maintain women's subordination and exploitation.

The study

Our research examined men's knowledge, attitudes, and behaviour in three areas fundamental to the social construction of masculinity: sexuality, reproduction, and fatherhood. It aimed to provide information which could be used for planning further work with men to help them develop an understanding of their role in the promotion of sexual and reproductive health. The study formed the first part of a pilot project to involve men in health promotion in their communities.

In all, 90 men were recruited for inclusion in the study, from five urban and three rural communities in different parts of Nicaragua where CISAS was already working with groups of women and children. They were aged from 15 to 70. Seventy per cent were married and/or living with their partners; 30 per cent were single. The average number of children fathered by each man was 4.7. Forty per cent of participants had been educated to primary level or less, 50 per cent had secondary education, and 10 per cent had tertiary education.

Work began with a workshop in August 1997. CISAS health educators invited 38 men from the communities mentioned above who had previously participated in CISAS activities (such as community meetings and discussion groups). During the workshop, participants discussed issues related to sexuality, fatherhood, and reproduction with health educators, in small groups and in plenaries. Participants also completed a biographical questionnaire which included questions about their values and practical experience of contraception and fatherhood.

Using the questionnaire results, a small team of CISAS staff put together a guide for in-depth interviews and focus-group discussions on the same key issues as the initial workshop. Participants for these were men from the CISAS target communities who had not participated in the workshop. Ten men were interviewed, two from each of the five regions where CISAS works, and five focus-group meetings (one in each region) were held with eight men in each group. CISAS health educators recruited men who had participated from time to time in CISAS activities such as discussion groups or community meetings.

Many men seem to find it liberating to discuss close relationships and sexuality with other men. After the workshop, and after almost every interview and focus-group discussion, participants thanked researchers for the opportunity to share their opinions about these rather intimate subjects with other men. Many commented that it was the first time in their lives they had had this opportunity.

In qualitative research, not only the content, but the context of what is said is important (Miller and Glasner 1997). In any verbal interaction, speakers assume that what is said will produce a particular reaction in the interlocutor (Potter 1997); if the reaction is not the desired one, the speaker will change or correct what he or she says. While some regard this problematic for researchers, because it implies that sociological research is always subject to contextual bias, others argue that it is very useful, since it shows how established norms influence people's behaviour (May 1993). In our research, participants contradicted themselves, or clarified their comments, when they were afraid that what they had expressed might cast aspersions on their masculinity, or on the image that they wanted to project as reasonable, rational, and caring people. These two inter-related sets of values underlie what was said, and informed the relationships between participants, and between participants and facilitators. The comments and opinions which appear below must be seen in this context.

Some results

Attitudes to sexuality

An important theme in the discussions about sexuality was the belief that male sexuality is governed by instinct, and that it is something 'wild' which men need to make an effort to control. In all focus groups, men expressed pride in their stereotypical image as sexually voracious conquerors of women and therefore 'real men'. Such comments indicate that the first thing every man does on meeting a woman is to evaluate her as a possible sexual conquest. According to participants, such an evaluation involves her *parametros físicos* (physical appearance) and, secondly, her marital status: 'Men, because they want to be *machos* say that "whatever goes into the broiler is meat"… I've had sex with cousins, not with aunts, you understand, you have to respect them a bit more'.

In focus groups, all participants spoke of their sexuality in terms of force and strength, and of female sexuality in terms of beauty and passivity. Participants stated that 'honest' women should not have opinions on what they want in sex: it is up to the man to know how to please them. While many participants pointed out that sexuality had much to do with how people communicate, none of the participants identified communication as an attribute that they felt they had, or that they desired, with their partners.

Focus-group participants were asked about the qualities of the ideal female partner. The consensus was that she has a beautiful body, but more importantly, that she is a cook and household manager, who is willing and able to serve her man faithfully and be a good mother to his children. The ideal male was seen as a worker who earns enough money to support his wife and children: his role is to provide financially for his family's needs. He does not drink, take drugs, or womanise. Despite this, 26 per cent of the men who attended the workshop reported having more than one partner 'at the moment'. In discussions in the focus groups, it became evident that it is not just seen as a man's right to have more than one partner, but also as an important expression of his sexuality: 'From the moment I meet a woman that I fancy, I'm thinking that I'll do something with her, I'm going to get to know her and have an adventure; I can't stop it, it's part of me'; and 'We're unfaithful by nature, I guess men are just born bad.'

In comparison, a woman's infidelity is considered to be a different thing altogether: women, unlike men, are not by nature unfaithful. Unfaithful women are therefore 'bad' women. This is a good example of the double morality which is a salient feature of Nicaraguan *machismo*. However, a woman's infidelity is not only a reflection of her wickedness but also of her husband's failure, who apparently cannot satisfy her sexually.

Men showed varying degrees of homophobia. To many in the study, homosexuality is 'against nature' and against 'God's will'. Homosexuality was regarded as an illness with a direct physical cause, such as a 'brain tumour' or a 'small penis'. Some believed that it could be caught, as though it were a sexually transmitted disease. Others saw homosexuality as a result of society's loss of values. During discussions on this topic in the workshop, several men pointed out that society's views condemning homosexuality had a direct impact on the way that they relate to other men. There are certain things that men cannot do without being singled out as *cochones* (a derogatory term for homosexual men). These were not, as might be expected, tasks seen as women's work: they relate, instead, to how men relate to each other. For example, a man cannot comment on the beauty of another man: 'I don't want to say in public or in private, "this guy is handsome, beautiful, pretty", because they'll mark me down as a queer'.

Discussions about lesbianism highlighted the fact that men's sexuality is centred on the penis and penetration, since many could not conceive of a sexual relationship without penetration. The participants of two groups took this to extraordinary lengths, believing with unshakeable confidence that lesbians have penises (albeit somewhat smaller ones than men: 'two to three inches'). Focus-group participants spent much time trying to identify a direct cause for lesbianism. Most felt that it was due to the failure of men to please women sexually, but this was generally seen as the woman's fault: she must be the kind of woman whom men cannot please.

Attitudes to reproduction

Men expressed the opinion that within a marriage or a stable relationship, it is a man's right to decide when a woman should have children. This was never stated directly, but it was implicit in many of the comments about contraception. Participants felt this was because they were the ones who would be expected to provide for the children. 87 per cent of workshop participants, and every focus group, were in favour of contraception. It was clear from focus-group and interview information that the main reason for participants' support of contraception was because it prevented them from having to take economic responsibility for unwanted children. As one man pointed out: 'For me, family planning is important. I wouldn't want to have anymore because of my condition. I'm poor and wouldn't like any more children'.

Despite this, using contraception is still seen as a sin, as could be seen clearly in comments from the 13 per cent of workshop participants who expressed opinions against it: 'It's a sin. You see, only God knows what a child's destiny is. If God wants a child, he makes one, it is a sin to prevent it.' Many participants referred to it as sinful even while justifying its use, as in this comment by a workshop participant: 'It's a sin but, for me, it's more sinful to bring a mountain of children into the world and not know what to do with them; having them crying of hunger and not being able to feed them. That's a bigger sin.'

Statistics about the number of men in Nicaragua who abandon their pregnant partners are not available, but there is a high incidence of female-headed households, at 31 per cent of all households (INEC 1999). Almost exclusively, men in the study saw financial problems as the reason for abandoning partners and children. However, many did say they felt strongly that it was 'unmanly' to run away from the responsibility: "As a man, you have to take the responsibility, whether it's your wife or your lover or whatever, you can't reject it. Even if you have two women, you have to hide it from the woman you live with. Denying the responsibility wouldn't be manly.'

Despite such views, the consensus from interviews and focus groups was that using contraception is not men's responsibility. Focus-group participants' knowledge of how the different methods worked was poor, even among men with higher levels of education. Most discussions centred on the condom, vasectomy, and female sterilisation, probably because these were seen to be the most controversial methods.

Publicity about condom use by CISAS and other organisations had clearly been received by men in the study. Several repeated the slogans from the publicity proudly, and without prompting, during the workshop. However, while men in the study knew that condoms could prevent HIV infection and unwanted pregnancy, there was general agreement that very few men use them. Different reasons were cited for this, including illiteracy, the fact that the woman was known to be an 'honest woman', and the fact that sex with condoms does not feel the same. Despite this, some 68 per cent of workshop participants reported that they had used condoms within the past six months. It became clear that men felt that the only women they needed to use condoms with were those whom they judged to be 'suspicious': women in bars, and women whose pasts they do not know. One interviewee summed up the majority view: 'when you see a very suspicious woman

you might use it, but, sometimes when you meet a woman, maybe who's engaged, but allows you do it, there's no need to use a preservative. You know, they just don't feel the same, it's like attaching a hose or something, you just don't feel right.'

Vasectomy was said to affect the character of the man, making him like a woman. This view expressed a fear which many seemed to feel, that losing their ability to father children would affect their manhood. Having said this, not all men were against vasectomy; a few said that they would have the operation, because it was a safe and sure method of contraception which would prevent them from having to take economic responsibility for more children. Only one man admitted that he had actually had the operation.

Female sterilisation, more than any other contraceptive method, made men suspect that their partners wanted to have sex with other men. In the questionnaire, participants' responses to questions about female sterilisation reveal widespread fear of women's infidelity. 29 per cent of respondents to the questionnaire agreed with the statement: 'After women have the operation, they look for other men to have sex with'. In discussions, even men who said that they were not against female sterilisation first alluded to, and then dismissed, the infidelity myth: 'if she wants to get sterilised it's because she's crazy, she wants to cheat on her husband, she wants to have one man and then another'.

Attitudes to abortion

Over 92 per cent of the men in the workshop regarded abortion as a sin. In the focus groups, women who have abortions were termed 'murderers'. Men were asked in the groups and interviews why they thought abortions happened: they cited medical reasons, but also understood that many abortions take place for social reasons, which include relationship and economic problems. In focus groups, the consensus was that abortions were the fault of irresponsible women, highlighting the fact that most men do not see contraception as their responsibility.

The situation is slightly different for young, unmarried women. Men do not expect them to be responsible or to be able to resist seduction. Unwanted pregnancies in unmarried young women were seen as resulting from loss of parental control, and especially of fathers' control. However, even in the case of young women, men's suggested solution was to have the child and give it away.

Attitudes to fatherhood

All men in the study who had children talked of feeling mature after the birth of their first children, as though fatherhood provides a man with an entrance into 'real' adulthood. For most, these feelings went hand-in-hand with the realisation that they were now responsible for the child's upbringing. One man explained that, after the birth of a child, men feel a mixture of joy and worry over how they will be able to cope financially with the extra burden: 'In the moment [when your child is just born] you feel great, but then, well, you know, you start thinking, you're broke, and it's also worrying.'

According to the participants in four focus groups, providing economically for children is a father's principal role. The other main paternal responsibility is teaching children how to behave. Men felt that this is done through teaching children important values, including the value of work, honesty, responsibility, and respect for one's elders. These two responsibilities, as provider and disciplinarian, were the only two mentioned; only one man spoke of 'giving love' as a paternal responsibility.

On the other hand, it was very obvious that most men in the study value the love of their children, and the time that they spend with them. In the questionnaire, over 95 per cent remarked that playing with their children was important to them.

In group discussions and interviews, many men talked with pride of their children's affection for them.

Most men in the study reported that they involved themselves 'from time to time' in practical child-care. Activities mentioned included feeding, bathing, dressing, and even washing and ironing clothes. However, day-to-day child-care was seen as a help and support for mothers, rather than as part of a father's role.

The men were asked about the content of the last conversation that they had had with their children. Almost all the men said that they had been giving advice; only one man reported a discussion about a topic which did not have to do with control or discipline. It would seem from this that fathers either lack skills to communicate with their children in other ways, or do not see the importance of this. Many said they find it particularly difficult to communicate with their daughters, and that they are often stricter with them than with their sons. The reason cited for this was that fathers need to be especially vigilant with their daughters, to prevent them from becoming pregnant. Relationships between fathers and their daughters were generally seen as more difficult. One possible reason for this may be that daughters are regarded as less valuable than sons. A daughter is not valueless, but it appears that her value lies in her ability to serve her family, and not in her as a human being. As one man said: 'When I realised that God had given me a girl, I said to myself, "at least I have a cook to make me tortillas".'

Insights from the research

In many studies, *machismo* and the ideas on which the concept is based tend to act as an explanation (and, occasionally, an excuse) for men's behaviour. However, using *machismo* as an explanation or excuse assumes that the concept shapes men's conduct. In fact, perhaps its main effect is to present Nicaraguan society with a stereotypical model of men's and women's behaviour, which individuals may or may not adhere to. The results of this research should not be seen as a picture of a single, objective Nicaraguan machismo operating in interpersonal relationships, but as a snapshot of complicated, endlessly changing relationships between participants, their partners, and their children, and between participants and researchers.

If the research has little predictive value for men's behaviour in the context of their relationships, because it cannot depict the context, or explain the behaviour of individual men in their relationships with women and children, why spend good money in a poor country to do it?

Challenging male hegemony

It is necessary, as well as morally defensible, to use development methods which are based on a commitment to empowerment and active participation. Norms of masculinity are so artificial, and so inhuman, that they need to be policed to maintain them (Formaini 1990). Institutions which do this policing include the church, the government, the media, the medical profession, and — most effectively — the family (Schifter and Madrigal 1996). Together, these institutions put into place a system of discipline which affects the social behaviour of individual men and women under male leadership or rule (Connell 1995). As feminists have contended, empowered individuals not only can challenge male hegemony and norms of gender relations, but also play a significant role in reformulating these relations, which would result in true emancipation (Holland and Ramazanoglu 1994).

Participatory methods based on a commitment to empowerment have rarely been applied to work which focuses on men as gendered beings. Much has been written on the need to focus on women's participation through use of women-only groups, as well as by facilitating their full involvement in mixed groups, but the suggestion that a powerful group such as men may require specific attention is new and challenging.

Persuading men to participate in health promotion

Agencies which are reluctant to work with men on issues concerning sexual and reproductive health (Stycos 1996) may justify this by saying that men have little or no interest in the theme. However, CISAS's experience is that men are very interested once they can be persuaded to take part. One reason for men's unwillingness to be recruited as participants in such projects as ours may be their perception that health promotion is women's work. Possibly, development agencies themselves have had a major influence in this perception, since few efforts have been made to involve men in proactive community-development programmes. Many men, and some development agencies, continue to view men's participation as unnecessary, and even counter-productive (Drennon 1998).

For some women, the proposition that there might be an agenda for promoting men's sexual health seems threatening. As Marge Berer (1996) points out, many women are suspicious of health planners' aim to increase men's participation in reproductive and sexual health, viewing this as part of a campaign which aims to win back power for men. It is possible that these fears are well grounded, as they are founded on the bitter experience of the 1960s sexual revolution which, for all its rhetoric of sexual freedom, did little to change the subordinate role that women play in most sexual relations with men (Hawkes 1996). This is supported by some evidence that men's involvement in family planning has actually increased men's control over the fertility of women, rather than resulted in women having more choice (Cornwall 1998). There is also a danger that efforts to get men to participate will take away funds from projects that target women and children, and will ultimately result in re-establishing a male dominated and orientated agenda (Berer 1996; Helzner 1996).

These warnings should not go unheeded. The setting and application of a men's agenda for sexual health promotion should not result in the curtailment of services for women because funds are being reallocated to men (AVSC International 1997), nor should it give men the keys to more subtle forms of domination and exploitation. Ultimately, as feminists have long realised, men's participation in the reformation of gender relationships is a two-edged sword. Kimmel and Mesner (1995) point out that by making the processes of patriarchy visible to men, there is a risk that they will learn new ways of maintaining or even increasing its power, rather than reforming the norms upon which it is based. The job of ensuring that this does not occur lies fairly, if not squarely, in the hands of professional health promoters working with men.

Peter Sternberg is a development worker employed by ICD/CIIR. He has worked with CISAS as a health educator and a researcher for the past four years. Contact details: Peter Sternberg, CISAS, Apartado Postal 3267, Managua, Nicaragua. E-mail: pms@ibw.com.ni

Notes

1 For a useful introduction to Nicaraguan social and political history up to 1990 see Norsworthy, K (1990) *Nicaragua: A country guide*, The Interhemispheric Education Resource Centre, Albuquerque, New Mexico.

2 For an interesting review (in Spanish) of the way the patriarchy handled the case see Huerta, JR (1998) *El Silencio del Patriarcha*, Renacimeinto, Managua.

References

AVSC International (1998) 'Men as Partners Initiative: Summary report of literature review and case studies', AVSC International, New York

Barker, G (1996) 'The misunderstood gender: Male involvement in the family and in reproductive and sexual health in Latin America and the Carribean', John D and Catherine T Macarthur Foundation, Chicago.

Baró MI (1988) *Acción e Ideología. Pscología Social de Centroamérica*, University of Central America (UCA), San Salvador, El Salvador.

Berer, M (1996) 'Men', *Reproductive Health Matters*, 7, May.

CENIDH (1998) 'Derechos Humanos en Nicaragua', Centro Nicaragüense de Derechos Humanos, Managua.

Connell R (1995) *Masculinities*, Polity Press/Blackwell, Oxford.

Cornwall, A (1998) 'Beyond reproduction: Changing perspectives on gender and health', *Bridge*, 7, available from http://www.ids.ac.uk/ids/research/bridge (accessed 31 January 1999).

Doyal, L (1991) 'Promoting women's health', in Badura B and Kickbusch I (eds) *Health Promotion Research*, WHO, Copenhagen.

Drennon, M (1998) 'Reproductive Health: New Perspectives on Men's Participation', Population Reports, Johns Hopkins University School of Public Health, Population Information Program, October.

Formaini, C (1990) *Men: The darker continent*, Heinemann, London

GHCV (1997) *Responsibilidad Masculina en Salud Sexual y Reproductiva*, Grupo de Hombres Contra la Violencia, RSMLAC, Si Mujer, Managua.

Hawkes, G (1996) *A Sociology of Sex and Sexuality*, Open University, Buckingham.

Helzner, J (1996) 'Men's involvement in family planning', *Reproductive Health Matters*, 7, 146–154, May.

Holland, J and Ramazanoglu, C (1994) 'Coming to conclusions: power and interpretation: researching young women's sexuality', in Maynard M and Purvis, J *Researching Women's Lives from a Feminist Perspective*, Taylor and Walker, London.

INEC (1999) 'Encuesta Nicaragüense de Demografía y Salud: 1998', Instituto Nacional de Estadístícas y Censos (INEC), Managua.

Kimmel, M, and Mesner, M (1995) 'Introduction' in Kimmel M, and Mesner M, (eds) *Men's Lives* (3rd edition), Allyn and Bacon Needham Heights, Mass.

Lancaster, R (1992) *Life is hard: Machismo, danger, and the intimacy of power in Nicaragua*, University of California, Berkeley.

Lize, S (1998) 'Masculinity and men's health needs: a Jamaican perspective', *Bridge*, 7, available from http://www.ids.ac.uk/ids/research/bridge (accessed 31 January 1999).

May, T (1993) *Social Research: Issues, methods and process*, Buckingham, Open University Press.

Miller J, and Glasner, B (1997) 'The "inside" and the "outside": finding realities in interviews', in Silverman, D (ed) (1997).

MINSA (1999) 'Plan Estratégico Nacional de Lucha Contra ETS/VIH/SIDA: Nicaragua 2000–2004', Ministry of Health of the Republic of Nicaragua, Managua.

Montenegro, S (1997) *La revolución simbólica pendiente: mujeres, medios de comunicación y política*, CINCO, Managua.

PASCA (1997) 'Resumen de País — la Situación del VIH/SIDA en Nicaragua', Proyecto Acción SIDA de Centro América (PASCA), Managua.

Pizarro, A (1996) *A Tu Salud*, SI Mujer, Managua.

Potter, J (1997) 'Discourse analysis as a way of analysing naturally occurring talk' in Silverman, D (ed) (1997).

Schifter, J and Madrigal, J (1996) 'Las Gavetas Sexuales del Costarricense y el Riesgo de Infeccion con el VIH', Editorial IMEDIEX, San Jose, Costa Rica.

Silverman, D (ed) (1997) *Qualitative Research: Theory, method and practice*, Sage, London.

Stycos, M (1996) 'Men, Couples and Family Planning: A retrospective look', Working Paper No 96,12, Cornell University Population and Development Program, Cornell University.

Vargas, O-R (1998) 'Pobreza en Nicaragua: un abismo que se agranda', Centro de Estudios de la Realidad Nacional (CEREN), Managua.

Vargas, O-R (1999) 'El Síndrome de Pedrarias', Centro de Estudios de la Realidad Nacional (CEREN), Managua.

Wegner, M, Landry, E, Wilkinson, D, and Tzanis, J (1998) 'Men as Partners in reproductive health: From Issues to Action', *International Family Planning Perspective*, 24:1, 38–42.

Welbourn, A (1995) 'Stepping Stones: A training package on HIV/AIDS, communication and relationship skills', ActionAid, London.

Wilton, T (1994) 'Feminism and the erotics of health promotion', in Doyal L, Naidoo, J and Wilton T (eds) *Women and AIDS: Setting a Feminist Agenda*, Taylor and Francis, London.

Women's health and HIV:
Experience from a sex workers' project in Calcutta

Madhu Bala Nath

In her job as Gender and HIV Adviser for UNAIDS/UNIFEM, the author came across a movement of sex workers who are successfully negotiating safe sex in the heart of Calcutta, India. This article relates an inspiring discovery for those development professionals who are searching for ways to empower women to protect themselves, their partners, and families from HIV infection.

During the last 20 years of the twentieth century, HIV/AIDS emerged as a major challenge to the health of millions, and ultimately to the development of the world. By the end of 2000, according to the projections of the World Health Organization (WHO), 40m men, women and children worldwide will be infected by HIV, or will have developed AIDS. The epidemic is in different stages of maturity in different parts of the world. It first manifested itself in sub-Saharan Africa and in the industrialised countries of the North during the 1980s, but is now rampaging in other areas of the world, including Asia. The years 1996 and 1997 saw a doubling of infection rates in 27 countries in Africa, in almost every country in Asia, and in some countries in Eastern Europe (UNAIDS 1998a).

HIV/AIDS in Asia

Sixty per cent of the world's people of reproductive age — assumed to be the age-span during which most sexual activity takes place — are located in Asia. Asia is a region of labour surplus, due to its youthful and rapidly growing demographic profile, and as such it has huge numbers of domestic and international migrants. Such mobile populations are known to be at a relatively high risk of contracting HIV (UNDP 1993). This demographic situation, along with existing, and in many cases increasing, gender inequalities in the region, has led to a scenario wherein out of the 2.7m estimated new HIV cases in the world in 1996, 1m were in south and south-east Asia (UNAIDS 1997). India is home to about 4m people living with HIV/AIDS. This is the largest number of infected individuals in any single country in the world (UNAIDS 1999).

The current rate of infections in India is very high. Between 1988 and 1989, in the north-eastern state of Manipur, none of the 2,322 injecting drug users recorded by the State AIDS Control Organisation tested positive for HIV. By June 1990, the rate of infection among them stood at 54 per cent, and at present is 77 per cent (Narain 1999). However, figures such as these show only the tip of the iceberg. It is thought that only 8 per cent of the infections in India have occurred through contaminated syringes for drug use, and a further 8 per cent through blood transfusions. About 75 per cent of the infections have been contracted through sexual contact (*Times of India*, 1 December 1999). In 1995, the WHO recorded 333m cases of sexually transmitted diseases (STDs) in the world, out of which 150m were in south and south-east Asia. The presence of STDs in the human body increases the risk of HIV transmission five-fold (ODA 1996). According to a behavioural survey financed by USAID in Tamil Nadu, India, 82 per cent of the chosen sample of male STD patients had had sexual intercourse with multiple partners within the previous 12 months, and only 12 per cent had used a condom (ODA 1996).

Although the links between gender identity and roles, sexual behaviour and HIV infection are complex, it is becoming more and more clear that gender-based discrimination is a central cause, and consequence, of the HIV/AIDS epidemic (UNDP 1990). The geographical locations where the epidemic is thriving are areas with serious economic, social and political inequality between women and men. In my work, piloting new and innovative approaches in various parts of the world to address the gender dimensions of the epidemic, I constantly search for answers to the questions raised again and again by women in their struggle to cope with the rapidly spreading epidemic. These questions include whether a woman can be assertive in her sexual relationship with a man.

For most Indian women, it is almost impossible to contemplate this. Women are brought up to rely on the principles of mutual fidelity in marriage, and *pati parmeswar* (the husband is God). Does reliance on these ideals create an illusion of safety for her, which will shape her attitude to risk? If a woman has no such illusions, how can she suggest safe sex by ensuring that her partner wears a condom, when the very suggestion of condom use carries with it an indication of infidelity that could threaten the security of not only the relationship but her very existence?

Sonagachi and the SHIP project

Amid the grim statistics on HIV and AIDS in India, the story I have to tell here is encouraging. It focuses on the sexual health and HIV intervention project in Sonagachi, a red-light area[1] in Calcutta, which I visited in August 1999. Some of the red-light areas in cities and towns in India have been recording a prevalence rate of HIV/AIDS as high as 55 per cent since 1996 (UNAIDS 1996). A recent study in India revealed that 90 per cent of the male clients of male sex workers were — reportedly — married (ODA 1996).

In visiting Sonagachi, I wanted to improve my understanding of the ways in which women, including women sex workers, are negotiating safer sexual practices, to prevent the spread of HIV and AIDS.[2] I did not get simple answers to my questions, but I did stumble upon a discovery: a movement of sex workers who are successfully negotiating safe sex in the heart of Calcutta. The information given in this article has been consolidated from information provided by the sex workers of Calcutta, through focus group discussions, informal interviews and visits to their homes during 1999. Further information comes from interviews I conducted with a number of clients of the sex workers, social workers working in the area, doctors working in the STD clinics, the donors supporting the Sonagachi project, and non-governmental organisations (NGOs) working in similar or related projects in other parts of Calcutta.

For the past 400 years, Sonagachi has been known as the area in Calcutta where vice and crime prevail. In a focus-group discussion, some of the sex workers reminisced about their lives in the area. Shankari Pal told me: 'We got only slaps. Shoes were thrown at us, cigarette butts were stubbed on our cheeks.' Stories are common of trafficking in young girls. It was usual for the services of sex workers to be bought through some kind of coercion. Women in Sonagachi told me that many of the most exploitative brothel owners — the *malkins* — had been the most vulnerable of sex workers themselves. One *malkin*, Bela didi, had lived in a bonded state of existence for ten years. Every penny she earned went to repay her 'debt'. The debt was the money the pimp had paid for her (approximately US$150) and the money for her keep, including provision of her clothes and cosmetics, and rent of an area 10ft by 10ft in the brothel, food, water, electricity, and medicines.

The first sex worker in Calcutta to test HIV-positive did so in 1982, in Kidderpore. Subsequently, other cases were detected, in adjoining red-light areas, including Sonagachi. In 1992, when the estimated prevalence rates among sex workers had risen to 5 per cent, the STD/HIV Intervention Project (SHIP) was set up by the All-India Institute of Hygiene and Public Health, a semi-autonomous government institution in Calcutta funded by the state government of West Bengal. Financial support was provided first by WHO and soon afterwards, by the Norwegian and British development agencies. Dr Samarjit Jana, an epidemiologist, was appointed project director.

The SHIP project was an experimental public health intervention, focusing on the transmission of STDs and HIV among communities in Calcutta. It set up an STD clinic for sex workers in Sonagachi, to promote disease control and condom distribution, in line with the then-popular approach of targeting HIV prevention to particular groups who were particularly at risk. However, during the course of the project, the focus broadened considerably beyond disease control, to address the structural issues of gender, class and sexuality. Brothels in Sonagachi were frequented by people from 'respectable' society, who took pains to avoid any possibility of recognition. Police brutality against sex workers was an enormous

problem. Life in the area laid bare power relations and resultant exploitation in the crudest form possible. Sonagachi is a community where constant negotiations are going on, and it was perhaps this aspect of life that inspired work to control HIV through addressing sexuality and gender power relations.

The SHIP project has three fundamental operating principles for its work: respect, recognition and reliance. The belief that sex workers are best working for themselves has informed its strategies. For example, 25 per cent of managerial positions have been reserved for sex workers, and sex workers hold key positions. This strategy was initiated by the charismatic leader of the project, Mrinal Kanti Dutta, who told me: 'Only if there is no alternative will outsiders be considered'. The child of a sex worker, Mrinal was born in an alley in Kalighat, a red-light area. To protect him from harassment, his mother sent him to a school in a neighbouring locality. However, this created problems of rootlessness: while Mrinal's education separated him from the offspring of other sex workers, his identity kept him ostracised from conventional society. He attributes his abilities as an activist to this unusual start in life.

The focus on using 'insiders' to work with their peers to motivate them reflects the ideology on which the project is based. From early on, members of the sex workers community were invited to act as peer educators, clinic assistants, and clinic attendants in the project's STD clinics. Mrinal was the first to join as a clinic attendant. Sixty-five female sex workers from the community were enrolled as peer educators. Since that start, SHIP has aimed to build sex workers' capacity to question the cultural stereotypes of their society, and build awareness of power and who possesses it. It seeks to do this in a way that is democratic and challenging, yet non-confrontational.

'Negotiating with the self'

The respect and recognition provided by the project to these peer educators transformed their lives. From the very beginning, the project made it clear to the sex workers that in no way would a 'rehabilitation' approach be adopted. The project had not been established to 'save' 'fallen women'. The peer educators were provided with a uniform of green coats, and staff identity cards, which gave them social recognition. A series of training activities were organised, with the aim of promoting self-reliance and confidence, and respect for them in the community. Comments from peer educators are on record in a project report. One reported: 'The project has enabled me to face society with confidence'; another said: 'This apron has changed my life, my identity. Now I can tell others that I am a social worker, a health worker' (DMSC 1998).

A base-line survey was conducted, using a participatory methodology. A series of group discussions were conducted, to debate the question, 'Why am I where I am?'. The survey confirmed that extreme economic poverty and social deprivation were the main factors driving women into the sex trade: 84.4 per cent of the sex workers were found to be illiterate; only 8.6 per cent of the sex workers had come willingly to the sex trade, and the rest were there because of acute poverty, a family dispute, or because of having been misguided or kidnapped (AIIHPH 1997).

Once the sex workers saw the results of the discussions and the survey statistics, they could see their vulnerability to structural problems, and those who had previously seen themselves as 'sinners' and 'loose women' changed their perspectives. In focus group discussions, peer educators told me:

'For us, this trade is also an employment. Why wouldn't the government recognise it? Who says we are loose women?'

'Are we alone to blame? What about the men who come to us? Are they not also polluting the society?'

'We give our art. In fact, we give a lot to this society — number-one quality stuff. The society has an obligation to give us respect in return. We are not begging, we do not seek rehabilitation as we are not disabled.'

This awakening is a very significant transformation that the project has achieved. The sex workers of Calcutta have begun to challenge the age-old notions of sin and blame, and are trying to reconstruct their identity. This perhaps, is the first stage of negotiations towards safer sexual practices — a negotiation with the self.

Negotiating with peers

It was a sad irony in the story of Sonagachi that, as women in the sex trade were engaged in building self-awareness and questioning unequal power, an incident occurred in the project area that brought their vulnerability home to them. In early September 1994, blood samples were forcibly collected from approximately 50 sex workers. This was carried out by an NGO with the help of the state government and the local police. Earlier, they had dragged out a brothel owner to the local police station and threatened her with serious consequences if she did not co-operate with them in these research trials (DMSC 1998).

Although the SHIP project had started well, the empowerment of 65 peer educators was not adequate to protect the 5,000 sex workers who lived in Sonagachi alone from this abuse of their rights. How could the project keep a focus on promoting safer-sex practices while the wider issue of political rights remained unaddressed? This incident proved to be a catalyst for the peer educators' understanding of the power relations surrounding sex work. They began to view the issue within a framework of human rights, and to feel that it was critical that an organised body of sex workers be set up to fight such assaults on their dignity and rights. From negotiations with the self, they moved to a new level: negotiations with their peers.

The peer educators began their work, going from house to house in the red-light areas, equipped with information on STD/HIV prevention, AIDS, how to access medical care, and ways of questioning power structures that promoted violence. House-to-house work took three hours each morning. Each day, every group of peer educators (four in each group) contacted between 40 and 50 sex workers, and between 10 and 15 brothel owners. They encouraged the sex workers to attend the clinic for regular health check-ups; they used flip charts and leaflets for effective dissemination of information on STDs and HIV; they carried condoms with them to distribute to the sex workers.

It was extremely important to visit all the brothels and promote a sense of community among them. This coming-together had a direct bearing on promoting safer sexual practices, since the clients soon found that at least in some clusters they could not move from one brothel to another in search of condom-free sex. The conditions were the same in all the brothels.

As the project progressed, the educators monitored the use of the condoms by encouraging the sex workers to dispose of them in cardboard boxes. When asked by researchers about the rate of condom use and whether it had shown signs of rising, educators said: 'Look at the dustbins in the area and you will get the answer. The cardboard boxes are there to show that the rate of condom use has definitely gone up' (DMSC 1998).

As these activities got underway, awareness grew in the community about the project. While the project had begun as a targeted intervention to prevent the spread of HIV/AIDS, using a strategy of promoting behavioural change, it had become clear to all involved that the main obstacles facing the successful implementation of the project were not just behavioural. They were to do with the way sexuality is seen in society, the lack of social acceptance of sex work, and the legal ambiguities relating to it. All these were now being increasingly recognised by the community as elements to be confronted, battled against and overcome. Sex work was an occupation, and not a moral condition. And because it was an occupation, the occupational hazards of STDs, HIV, violence, and sexual exploitation had to be acknowledged as such, and overcome.

Building alliances with the clients

In 1993, early in the life of the project, a survey was conducted by the peer educators with *babus* (long-term, regular clients). The survey revealed that only 51.5 per cent of the clients had heard of HIV/AIDS, but even this group lacked awareness regarding the use of condoms. Only 1.5 per cent regularly used condoms, and 72.7 per cent had never used a condom (AIIHPH 1997). After the survey, a meeting was organised, to begin to build alliances between sex workers and their regular clients in the interest of promoting safer sexual practice. About 300 clients attended. The discussions that began at this meeting led to the opening of evening clinics for the clients, where they could receive free treatment, counselling and access to condoms. Socio-cultural programmes were organised to introduce safer sex and HIV/AIDS messages targeting the clients. Today, the clients have come together in a support group called the Sathi Sangha ('Group of Friends'). This group supports the sex workers in motivating new clients to use condoms, and supports the sex workers' efforts to eliminate sexual violence in the area.

Training the police

A training session for police personnel was organised, after a strong partnership had been established, between the project and the Calcutta Police Department, by the All-

India Institute of Health and Hygiene. By the end of April 1996, about 180 police officers had attended these training programmes.

Forming the DMSC

The issue of HIV/AIDS, which was the entry-point for work in Sonagachi, had become a starting-point for social transformation. An organisation for sex workers, the Durbar Mahila Samanvaya Committee (DMSC), was formed in February 1995. DMSC is a fully-fledged union for sex workers, promoting and enforcing their rights. A leading daily newspaper, the *Ananda Bazar Patrika*, hailed this move with the headline, 'Sex workers form their own organisation'. The leader of SHIP, Mrinal Kanti Dutta, was involved in the development of DMSC from the start. The sex workers in Sonagachi had graduated to becoming vociferous advocates for legislation for the recognition of their work as a profession.

The move was hailed because it was radically different from earlier attempts. Many organisations attempting to bring sex workers together call themselves fallen women's organisations.[3] These attempts have disallowed new notions of self and only serve to enhance guilt and shame amongst their members. Abha Bhaiya has very aptly remarked that 'such attempts have been apologetic rather than liberating', and have remained peripheral to mainstream women's movements (internal UNIFEM report, 1999).

On the day that Mrinal became the head of the DMSC — 1 May 1999 — the organisation won its first major political victory. This was formal recognition on the part of the state government of the self-regulatory boards that DMSC's members had set up together with officials from the Department of Social Welfare and the state's Women's Commission. These boards outline a mutually agreed code of conduct for all stakeholders in the red-light areas of West Bengal and with the help of the peer educators, who monitor activities closely, ensure that this code of conduct is adhered to.

Learning points

Using stories and history to rally the community

Part of the success of the Sonagachi story depends on the fact that, historically, there was a vitality in the sex workers' community. In 1980, a group of sex workers had formed Mahila Sangha (literally, 'women's organisation'). Braving threats, they carried on a sustained campaign against a local criminal who extorted money from the sex workers, finally driving him away (DMSC 1998). When the SHIP project started, the peer educators were able to use stories of these earlier successes to stir people's emotions and rally them round a common objective. Another shared memory assisted work with the sex workers' clients: that of the significant role played by a group of *babus* in the history of prostitution in Calcutta. During the days of the nationalist struggle against colonialism in India in the early twentieth century, these *babus* had inspired the Sonagachi women to raise funds to aid the freedom struggle.

Retaining flexibility, meeting changing needs

The SHIP project tried to respond to the perceived needs of sex workers in Sonagachi, as and when they arose. For example, although it began by solely focusing on the sex workers' sexual health needs, it made arrangements to provide them with non-formal education when the demand for literacy programmes arose. Similarly, vocational training programmes were conducted for older sex workers during 1996 — 97 in response to their concerns about security in old age. A credit and savings society, the Usha Multipurpose Society, was established, to help former sex workers to set up self-employment schemes. This component also aimed to liberate the community at large from the exorbitant rates of interest charged by money-lenders. More and more women joined as they found the process meeting their needs The report of the DMSC published in June 1998 states that 2000 sex workers had enrolled as members and that the assets of the co-operative amounted to Rs. 697,100 ($17,000), as well as a piece of land in Madhyamgram, the market price of which was Rs 8,000,000 ($200,000).

Using drama to promote communication

Opportunities for communication and self-expression have been created by the sex workers themselves, through Komal Gandhar theatre group. Communicating about methods of negotiating safe sex is critical, and drama has enabled the sex workers to negotiate publically with the clients, the pimps, the *malkins* and the police, in a non-threatening environment. Sex workers stated: 'It has given us the space to say things that reside in our hearts', and 'This medium has been very effective in improving [the use of] a code of health conduct by our clients'.

Negotiating with men and opposing patriarchy

The project has a philosophy of fighting patriarchy rather than individual men. In addition, there are groups of men who can be enlisted to work with women if there are mutual benefits. For example, the sex workers enlisted the support of clients to fight HIV infection to their mutual benefit. In 1993, a team of sex workers from the project met with the *mukhiya* (chief of the pimps) to negotiate his support. It became clear that the *mukhiya* did not want to support the project, because he feared that recognising that the HIV virus was present in Sonagachi would destroy their business. The project team explained that what would destroy the business was in fact

turning a blind eye to the spread of AIDS. The pimps have not resisted the campaign. Similar approaches were adopted with the police and *malkins,* who benefit from patriarchal power structures.

The success of police training sessions can be seen in the comments of peer educators, who reported to me: 'The police have to think twice before hitting us' and 'Today, we go to the police station and we are offered a chair to sit on. Earlier, they did not even register a case if we went to report abuse.' The *malkins* have also responded to the project. A number of them today keep condoms and provide these to the *babus* as they arrive. Some provide days off for the *chokris* (young sex workers), especially during menstruation. This was not the case a few years ago. Bela Didi, the *malkin* discussed earlier in this article, informed us that she had opened an account in the Usha Co-operative Society for her *chokris*.

From the periphery to the centre

Development work has tended to shy away from addressing issues of sex and sexuality. In the last two decades, HIV/AIDS has forced many policy-makers and practitioners to venture into this area, but the discomfort that most of them feel has kept the discussion at very preliminary levels. It is rare that the need for transformation of perceptions about sex, and attitudes related to morality and values, are discussed. The SHIP project is unusual and inspiring because it did this, with the aim of transforming and reforming power relations between women and men, and sex workers and those who profit from their work — both buyers and sellers. The project was seen by Abha Bhaiya, a consultant for UNIFEM who visited the project in August 1999, as a unique example of a community being mobilised to use human resources in a public health/AIDS control intervention (internal UNIFEM report, 1999).

Over the past seven years, the SHIP project has regularly celebrated International Women's Day, World Environment Day, and World AIDS Day, participated in book fairs and in flood relief programmes, sent delegations to Nepal and Bangladesh, and to World AIDS conferences. The sex workers have met with a range of partners, and have developed the view that their struggle as sex workers is not very different from the struggles of poor women in the informal sector. The struggles are against patriarchy and domination. Certain nuances in these struggles are different, but the overall spirit and thrust remain the same. Both the struggles have questioned power relations, both have explored and identified vulnerabilities, both have tried to break structures that are oppressive.

The sex workers of Sonagachi have today re-examined their situation vis-à-vis mainstream society, and have come up with some very powerful observations and insights. One, Mala Sinha, referred in a focus group to the women in mainstream society as well as the sex workers of her community as 'Dogs — it's just that one is a dog with a collar and one is without it.' Another, Minoti Dutt, remarked: 'We are more liberated and free in many ways. Those husbands as passports to our identity are irrelevant' (internal UNIFEM report, 1999).

The Sonagachi movement has also successfully intervened in stopping child trafficking in West Bengal. The self-regulatory boards set up in 1999 are the mechanism that enforce this. A number of children trafficked have been returned to their homes, and in this way the organisation is reducing vice and violence in wider society.

Conclusion: the value of dreams

The sex workers of Sonagachi dreamt a dream seven years ago, of having a community without violence, oppression, HIV or other STDs. But this dream did not fit into the larger development context of India or the Asian region. In 1992, India was embarking on its second medium-term plan for AIDS control, and WHO's epidemiological analysis forecast a bleak picture. By 1994, at the World AIDS Conference in Yokohama, India was being projected as the future AIDS capital of the world. Studies of high-risk behaviour commissioned by the National AIDS Control Organisation in 65 cities of India in 1994–95 only validated and confirmed this diagnosis. A survey of randomly selected households in Tamil Nadu found that, even in this small state, close to half a million people were infected with HIV. Since nearly 10 per cent of the people surveyed had STDs, HIV clearly had fertile ground on which to spread rapidly (UNAIDS 1998).

The existence of such factors made the dream of the women of Sonagachi seem rather unreal. But by 1996, research from SHIP showed indicators that were very different from four years before (AIIHPH 1997; DMSC 1998). Knowledge of STDs in Sonagachi improved from 69 per cent in 1992 to 97.4 per cent in 1996; knowledge of HIV/AIDS rose from 30.7 per cent to 96.2 per cent in the same period; and condom usage shot up from 2.7 per cent to 81.7 per cent in 1996. HIV/AIDS prevalence levels plateaued at 5 per cent, when other red-light areas the country were recording a rate of 55 per cent. In fact, the *Telegraph*, a leading daily newspaper, hailed Sonagachi as as having a negative growth rate of HIV/AIDS, despite being the 'biggest brothel in Asia' (*Telegraph*, 18 September 1995).

In conclusion, the dream has only partly been fulfilled. Sonagachi's women told me that they were still dreaming of a world where sex work would be recognised as legitimate work, and where sex workers have been able to choose it freely as a choice among other choices. A majority of the workers I met would like to enter

108

stable marital relationships, and they want the world to have re-defined sex and sexuality from a feminist perspective.

I left Sonagachi with a number of visions in my mind — an oasis in a desert, a flickering flame in a storm, a mountaineer scaling heights.

Madhu Bala Nath is Gender and HIV Adviser for UNAIDS/UNIFEM, 304 East 45 Street, 15th Floor, New York, NY 10017, USA; e-mail: madhu.bala.nath@undp.org / naths3940@aol.com

Notes

1 Red-light area: an area where sex-workers live and work.
2 I should state here that the relationship between HIV transmission and sex work is complex, and it is essential to avoid demonising sex workers by blaming them for the spread of HIV. Recognition must be given to the unequal power relations that exist between a sex worker, her/his client, and any other sexual partners the client may have.
3 For example, Patita Udhar Samiti, which means 'an organisation to save fallen women'.

References

All India Institute of Hygiene and Public Health (1997) 'A dream, a pledge, a fulfilment: A report on the SHIP project 1992-1997'.

Bloom and Lyons (1993) *Economic Implications of AIDS in Asia*, UNDP, New York.

DMSC (Durbar Mahila Samanwaya Committee) (1998) 'The fallen learn to rise: A report on the social impact of SHIP'.

Adler, M, Foster, S, Richens, J, and Slavin, H (1996) 'Sexual health and care: Sexually transmitted infections – Guidelines for prevention and treatment', ODA Health and Population Occasional Paper, ODA, London.

Narain JP (1999) *HIV/AIDS and Sexually Transmitted Diseases: An update*, WHO, Geneva.

Gordon, Peter and Sleightholme, Carolyne (1996) 'Review of Best Practice for Targeted Interventions: Second draft report submitted to Health and Population Office, Development Cooperation Office, Delhi, India', International Family Health, London.

Reid, E (1990) *Placing Women at the Centre of the Analysis*, UNDP, New York.

Solon, O and A Barrozo, (1993) 'Overseas contract workers and the economic consequences of HIV/AIDS in the Philippines', in Bloom and Lyons (1993).

UNAIDS (1996) *UNAIDS Fact Sheet*, UNAIDS, New York.

UNAIDS (1997) *Report of the Global HIV/AIDS Epidemic*, UNAIDS, New York

UNAIDS (1998a) *Intensifying the Global Response to the HIV/AIDS Epidemic*, UNAIDS, New York.

UNAIDS (1998b) 'AIDS Epidemic Update December 1998', UNAIDS, New York.

UNAIDS (1999) *The UNAIDS Report: A Joint Response to AIDS*, UNAIDS, New York.

Resources

Compiled by Erin Murphy Graham

This collection of resources is very wide-ranging, since it attempts to encompass the 'Gender in the Twenty-first Century' theme. Resources are arranged thematically within each sub-section.

Publications

The Globalization Reader (2000) Frank J. Lechner and John Boli (eds.), Blackwell Publishers.
108 Cowley Road, Oxford OX4 1JF, UK.
The various academic and political positions on globalisation and its implications for different regions are well covered in this comprehensive and accessible reader.

Economic Development and Women in the World Community (1996) Kartik C Roy, Clement A Tisdell, and Hans C Blomqvist (eds), Praeger.
88 Post Road West, Westport, CT 06881, USA.
This book explores the relationship between economic development and the socio-economic status of women in both developed and less developed countries. It argues that, given the benefits of greater economic independence and lower fertility rates on development, women are the most important agents of change. Case studies include developed regions, as well as Latin America and the Caribbean, sub-Saharan Africa, Malaysia, and China.

Women, Work, and Gender Relations in Developing Countries: A global perspective (1996) Parvin Ghorayshi and Claire Bélanger (eds), Greenwood Press.
88 Post Road West, Westport, CT 06881, USA.
Drawing on case studies, this book discusses theoretical and methodological considerations of gender relations and work, and linkages between the global economy and everyday life. It challenges the capitalist development paradigm and considers how empowerment and self-organisation promote social change.

Beyond Economic Man: Feminist theory and economics (1993) Marianne A Ferber and Julie A Nelson (eds), University of Chicago Press.
5801 South Ellis, Chicago, IL 60637, USA.
Economists, sociologists, and philosophers examine the central tenets of economics from a feminist point of view. Contributors discuss the extent to which gender has influenced both the range of subjects economists have studied and the way in which scholars have conducted their studies. The aim of this book is not to reject current economic practices, but to broaden them, permitting a fuller understanding of economic phenomena.

Feminist Economics: Interrogating the masculinity of rational economic man (1999) Gillian J Hewitson, Edward Elgar Publishers. Marston Book Services Ltd, PO Box 269, Abingdon, Oxon OX14 4YN, UK.

This book discusses the male biases inhererent in economists' debates on 'rational economic man' and reveals the implications, both theoretical and practical, of including women in mainstream economic thought.

The Elgar Companion To Feminist Economics (1999) Janice Peterson and Margaret Lewis (eds), Edward Elgar Publishers.

This recently published book includes 102 entries by 89 authors on a variety of topics relating to feminist economics.

The Economics of Women, Men and Work (1997) Francine Blau, Marianne A Ferber and Anne E Winkler, Prentice Hall Business Publishing, United States.

Tel: +1 1800 643 5506, Fax: +1 1800 835 5327.

This book is an introduction to current research on women, men, and work both in the labour market and the household. Particular attention is given to the changing roles of men and women in an increasingly globalised society.

The Economics of Gender (1998) Joyce P Jacobsen, Blackwell Publishers.

Introducing new work on the differences between women's and men's economic opportunities, activities, and rewards, this book explores questions such as why women earn less and why, throughout the world, men and women have tended to work in separate spheres. Although the primary focus is on contemporary patterns in the USA, four chapters compare a range of societies.

'Globalisation, employment, and gender' (1999) Süle Özler, in *Globalisation with a Human Face: United Nations Human Development Report 1999 Background Papers Vol. I*, UNDP.

United Nations Publications, 1 UN Plaza, New York, NY, 10017, USA.

This paper provides a review of the literature on globalisation and women's work. Using additional survey data from Turkey and Columbia, the paper argues that the effects of globalisation on employment are not gender-neutral, and that women are increasingly represented in the workforce. Among the implications given are women's increased empowerment in the family and community, and increased decision-making in the areas of economics, fertility, and family mobility.

Women and Empowerment: Participation in decision-making (1995) Marilee Karl, Zed Books.

7 Cynthia Street, London N1 9FJ, UK.

This book attempts to promote women's participation in civil society at the grassroots and international levels by providing an overview of what participation and empowerment mean and how they can be realised. One chapter looks specifically at the international mobilisation of women in and around the United Nations. The book concludes by outlining challenges that women face in increasing their participation and decision-making capacities.

Feminism and the New Democracy: Re-siting the political (1997) Jodi Dean (ed), Sage Publications.

A collection of essays which explore and respond to the debate about the relationship between politics and feminism. It attempts to offer a framework for the future of feminist theory and articulate a 'new democracy' that views the 'political' as complex and multi-faceted. Individual chapters address questions of ethnicity, culture, and sexual orientation.

Women, International Development, and Politics: The bureaucratic mire (1997) Kathleen Staudt (ed), Temple University Press. Broad & Oxford Streets, Philadelphia, Pennsylvania 19122, USA.

The contributors to this volume come from a variety of countries and work experiences, including Africa, Europe, Latin America, and the Middle EaSt Each contribution explores how women have been excluded from the democratisation process in many countries and analyses the influence of gender on the bureaucratic process. This volume also explores how NGOs continue to widen the public policy agenda to incorporate gender concerns.

The Challenge of Local Feminisms: Women's movements in global perspective (1995) Amrita Basu (ed), Westview Press.
Rejecting the notion that feminism is a Western-inspired concept of middle-class origins, this book provides an overview of the birth, growth, achievements, and dilemmas of women's movements worldwide, devoting attention mainly to Asia, Africa, and Latin America. It argues that women's movements are not necessarily able to transcend national differences, but are shaped by national levels of development.

Subversive Women: Women's movements in Africa, Asia, Latin America and the Caribbean (1995) Saskia Wieringa (ed), Zed Books Ltd.
An anthology of feminist writings from India, Indonesia, Peru, Somalia, Sudan, and the Caribbean, this book provides a historical perspective on women's organising. Individual chapters explore forms of resistance and social action including rebellion, unions, popular theatre, and poetry.

Moving from Accommodation to Transformation: New horizons for women into the 21st century (1997) Report of the Second African Women's Leadership Institute, Bisi Adeleye-Fayemi and Algresia Akwi-Ogojo (eds), Akina Mama wa Afrika.
4 Wild Court, London WC2B 4AU, UK.
The second AWLI meeting explored themes such as domestic violence, women's rights to political participation, women's reproductive health, and adolescent sexual behaviour in Nigeria. This booklet contains the abstracts of discussion papers, reports from training workshops and thematic discussion groups, and a final evaluation.

Organising Women: Formal and informal women's groups in the Middle East (1997) Dawn Chatty and Annika Rabo (eds), Berg.
150 Cowley Road, Oxford OX4 1JJ, UK.
This book analyses the relationship between the state and both women and men. It presents a mix of theoretical and empirical research that explores the informal and formal ways in which women have been organised and organised themselves in Arab societies. Ten articles present information gathered from Morocco, Egypt, Kuwait, Amman, and Lebanon.

Women and Social Movements in Latin America: Power from below (1997) Lynn Stephen, University of Texas Press.
Box 7819, Austin, TX 78713-7819, USA.
Six cases of women's grassroots activism, in El Salvador, Mexico, Brazil, and Chile, are presented in this book. Each case study analyses how these movements have combined women's concerns about survival and their oppression by men, and includes interviews with activists.

The Women, Gender, and Development Reader (1997) Nalini Visvanthan, Lynn Duggan, Laurie Nisonoff, and Nan Wiegersma (eds), Zed Books Ltd.
This reader contains over 30 articles exploring a number of themes relating to gender and development. It is organised into five sections focusing on theories of women; gender and development, households, and families; women in the global economy; women in the context of international social transformation; and women organising for change.

Women in the Third World: An encyclopaedia of contemporary issues (1998) Nelly P Stromquist (ed), Garland Publishing.
Taylor and Francis, 47 Runway Road, Suite G, Levittown, PA 19057, USA.
This reference work contains over 50 articles by more than 80 international experts on gender issues. The book encompasses a broad range of topics including political participation, human rights, housework, the family, equality, domestic and sexual violence, new jobs and exploitation in industrial production, AIDS, the gender consequences of ecological devastation, women's movements, education, and women in the media. It also contains an annotated bibliography of resources, the Convention on the Elimination of All Forms of Discrimination Against Women, and the Beijing Declaration.

A Passion for Difference (1994) Henrietta L Moore, Polity Press.
65 Bridge St, Cambridge, CB2 1UR, UK.
The theoretical section of this book develops a specific anthropological approach to current feminist post-structuralist and psychoanalytic theory. The following chapters explore related themes including gender; identity; violence, gender and identity in the household; and the links between the gender of the anthropologist and the writing of anthropology.

Feminism/Postmodernism/Development (1995) Marianne H Marchand and Jane L Parpart (eds), Routledge.
11 New Fetter Lane, London EC4P 4EE, UK.
This book explores the power struggle between voices from the South that challenge Northern control over development in a globalising world, where the meaning and practice of development are increasingly contested. It argues that issues such as identity, representation, indigenous knowledge, and political action must be incorporated into development

thought and practice. It includes examples of the experiences of women in Africa, Latin America, and Asia, as well as of women of colour in industrialised countries.

Feminist Visions of Development: Gender analysis and policy (1998) Cecile Jackson and Ruth Pearson (eds), Routledge.
This volume brings together articles from the leading scholars and activists in the gender and development field. It explores issues such as gender and the environment, education, population, reproductive rights, industrialisation, macroeconomic policy, and poverty. It is a comprehensive volume, relevant for students, academics, activists, and practitioners.

'Rethinking gender planning: A critical discussion of the use of the concept of gender' (1998) Saskia Wieringa, Institute of Social Studies Working Paper Series No. 279.
Publications Office, ISS, PO Box 29776, 2502LT The Hague, The Netherlands.
This article discusses the origins of the concept of gender, stressing its radical and comprehensive elements. It argues that the concept of gender has been 'watered-down', that women's issues have become de-politicised, and that concern for women's issues has been reduced to the socio-economic components of women's lives.

Women's Information Services and Networks: A global sourcebook (1999) Royal Tropical Institute, Oxfam GB, and International Information Centre and Archives for the Women's Movement, Kit Press and Oxfam.
BEBC, PO Box 1496, Parkstone, Dorset BH12 3YD, UK.
This sourcebook is a guide to women's organisations and networks around the world. It contains regional chapters on Africa, Asia, and the Pacific region, as well as central and eastern Europe. It provides brief descriptions and contact details of more than 160 organisations.

113

Women in Grassroots Communication: Furthering social change (1994) Pilar Riaño (ed), Sage Publications.
6 Bonhill St, London EC2A 4PU, UK.
Authors from Africa, Asia, and Latin America have contributed to this volume, providing a detailed analysis of women in grassroots communication in the developing world. The first section reviews various frameworks that address the relationship between women, communication, and participation. The second section analyses women's ability to communicate and the informal networks through which they do so at the local level. The third section focuses on media production and issues of media representation, evaluation, and competency. The final chapters explore issues of leadership, organisation, and communication strategies.

Women's Experiences in Media (1996) Rina Jimenez-David, ISIS International-Manila and the World Association for Christian Communication.
PO Box 1873, Quezon City Main, Quezon City 1100, The Philippines.
The second book to come from the 'Women Empowering Communication' conference in Bangkok, Thailand, Women's Experiences in Media presents an overview of recent developments and includes narratives of the initiatives that came out of the conference.

Women in the Media (1995) Margaret Gallagher, United Nations Department of Public Information.
UN Publications, 1 UN Plaza, New York, NY, 10017, USA.
This booklet contains general information on women in the media, focusing on women's under-representation and how increased female participation and inclusion can have a positive impact on gender inequality. Also included are 'success stories' of women from around the world who have made outstanding contributions in the media.

Women Empowering Communication: A resource book on women and the globalisation of media (1994) Margaret Gallagher and Lilia Quindoza-Santiago (eds), World Association for Christian Communication.
357 Kennington Lane, London SE11 5QY, UK.
The regional commentaries in this book highlight the situation of women with respect to the media around the world, concluding that the power to develop media policy and to determine media content continues to evade women. Chapters focus on women and the media in North America, Africa, Asia, Europe, the Middle East, and the Pacific region.

Men, Masculinity and the Media (1992) Steve Craig (ed) Sage Publications.
Bringing together scholars from the fields of communication studies, sociology, social studies, and political science, this volume looks at how the media constructs male identities and male relationships. The first section is a study of previous media research on men and masculinities, followed by sections presenting case studies and analysis of written and visual materials.

Men, Work and Family (1993) Jane C. Hood (ed), Sage Publications.
This anthology explores the diversity and complexity of men's work and their relationships with their families. Specific articles focus on Mexican American, Japanese, and Swedish men. The first chapter provides a theoretical overview and critique of men as 'providers' for the family. Other topics include single fatherhood and 'family-supportive' employment policies.

The Making of Anti-Sexist Men (1994) Harry Christian, Routledge.
This book presents the life stories of a group of 'pro-feminist' men which were explored through qualitative interviews. The first section of the book presents an analysis of the interview content and a

theoretical introduction to the study. It then relates the personal life stories of the eight men and explores the study's implications for the potential of men's participation in feminist struggles.

Men, Gender Divisions, and Welfare (1998) Jennie Popay, Jeff Hearn, and Jeanette Edwards (eds.), Routledge.
This volume explores the relationship between men and welfare, focusing on the persistence of men's power and men's avoidance of welfare services. Individual chapters discuss family matters, including 'Are men good for the welfare of women and children?' and '"I'm just a bloke who has kids": Men and women on parenthood'. The book brings together empirical studies, theoretical overviews, and analysis of contemporary discourse on masculinities.

Women Coping with HIV/AIDS: We take it as it is (1998) J van Woundenberg, Kit Press.
P.O. Box 95001, 1090 HA Amsterdam, The Netherlands.
This book is a medical anthropological study that explores the coping strategies of women with HIV/AIDS through in-depth interviews. Particular attention is given to how HIV/AIDS affects relationships and socio-economic conditions.

Triple Jeopardy: Women and AIDS (1990) The Panos Institute, Panos Publications.
9 White Lion Street , London N1 9PD, UK.
This book discusses ways in which HIV/AIDS threatens women: they may become infected themselves, pass the infection on in pregnancy, or carry the main burden of care if a family member is infected. *Triple Jeopardy* also explores the effect of AIDS on families and communities.

Women and HIV/AIDS: An international resource book (1993) Marge Berer with Sunanda Ray, Pandora Press.
77-85 Fulham Place Road, Hammersmith, London W6 8JB, UK.

The material in this book draws on a wide range of published and unpublished sources, bringing together knowledge and experience of HIV/AIDS from a woman-centred perspective. Topics explored include women's organisations, women's health and reproductive rights, and details of projects and services for women with HIV/AIDS. It is of interest to health activists and professionals, service providers, educators, researchers, and policy-makers.

'Women, HIV/AIDS and development: Towards gender-appropriate strategies in South East Asia and the South Pacific' (1992) Sally Baden, BRIDGE Report No.5, Institute for Development Studies, University of Sussex.
University of Sussex, Brighton, BN1 9RE, UK
This report provides an overview of the gender implications of HIV/AIDS in the South Pacific and South East Asia, particularly in terms of prevention and control strategies. The report points out the increasing number of heterosexual women who are infected with HIV/AIDS, and includes statistical information for the two regions. It suggests strategies for prevention and control.

'An investigation of community-based communication networks of adolescent girls in rural malawi for HIV/STD prevention' (1994) Deborah Helitzer-Allen, International Centre for Research on Women.
1717 Massachusetts Avenue, NW, Suite 302, Washington DC, 20036, USA.
This study investigates the feasibility of using traditional communication channels within rural communities for HIV/AIDS prevention initiatives. It explores adolescent girls' awareness of HIV/AIDS; their sources of information and social networks related to sex, marriage, and STDs and HIV/AIDS; the reported and actual sexual social norms; and the significance of ritual initiation ceremonies in sexual behaviour and knowledge.

'"I want to play with a woman": Gender relations, sexuality, and reproductive health in rural Zambia' (1995) Paul Dover, Development Studies Unit Working Paper No.29, Department of Social Anthropology, Stockholm University.
Stockholms Universitet, Annex 1, S-106 91, Stockholm, Sweden.
Based on a field study in Chiawa and Goba, using semi-structured interviews, this paper explores how sexuality relates to upbringing and gender roles, sexual practice, traditional marriage, and reproductive health including knowledge of HIV/AIDS and STD prevention.

Empowerment and Women's Health: Theory, methods, and practice (1998) Jane Stein, Zed Books.
Targeting both researchers and practitioners, this book analyses the relationship between women's empowerment and health. While it does not focus on HIV/AIDS in particular, its analysis makes links between international development policies, women's situations, and the theories of women's health issues.

My Gender Workbook: How to become a real man, a real woman, or something else entirely (1998) Kate Bornstein, Routledge.
This book's author identifies herself as 'transgendered'. The book explores gender issues from a personal, non-academic perspective, and includes gender quizzes and exercises to engage readers to think about their own gender identity. It is a unique and challenging addition to the gender studies literature.

The Lesbian and Gay Studies Reader (1993) H Abelove, MA Barale, and D Halperin (eds), Routledge.
This multi-disciplinary anthology contains more than 40 essays that illustrate the scope and diversity of the work currently being done in the field of lesbian and gay studies.

Feminism Meets Queer Theory (1997) Elizabeth Weed and Naomi Schor, Indiana University Press.
No reviews were traceable at the time of going to press.

Organisations

Women Working Worldwide, MITER, Room 126, MMU Humanities Building, Rosamond Street West, Manchester M15 6LL, UK.
Tel: +44 (0)161 247 1760
Fax: +44 (0)0161 247 6333
E-mail: women-ww@mcr1.poptel.org.uk
Website: www.poptel.org.uk/women-ww
Women Working Worldwide is a UK-based organisation started in 1983, which supports the struggles of women workers in the global economy through information exchange and international networking.

International Program for More and Better Jobs for Women (WOMEMP), International Labour Organization, Geneva, Switzerland.
Tel: +41 (0)22 799 8276 or +41 (0)22 799 7039
Fax:+41 (0)22 799 7657
E-mail: womemp@ilo.org
Website: www.ilo.org/public/english/employment/gems/conf/index.htm
The mission of this branch of the ILO is to promote employment in conditions of equality, and also to contribute to the successful follow-up to the Fourth World Conference on Women and the gender dimensions of the World Summit for Social Development. It also aims to assist in the development and implemention of national action plans to improve the quantity and quality of women's employment.

Womankind Worldwide, 3, Albion Place, Galena Road, London W6 0LT, UK.
Tel: +44 (020) 8563 8607
Fax: +44 (020) 8563 8611
E-mail: info@womoankind.org.uk
The organisation works with international partners in grassroots community work, and

in an international advocacy capacity, targeting the UK, EU, and UN, and informing the general public.

The Centre for Women's Global Leadership, Douglass College, Rutgers, The State University of New Jersey,160 Ryders Lane, New Brunswick, NJ 08901-8555, USA.
Tel: +1 (0)732 932 8782; fax: +1 (0)732 932 1180
E-mail: cwgl@igc.org
Website: www.cwgl.rutgers.edu
The Centre runs programmes to promote the leadership of women and advance feminist perspectives in policy-making processes in local, national, and international arenas. Since 1990, the Centre has worked to foster women's leadership in the area of human rights through women's global leadership institutes, strategic planning activities, international mobilisation campaigns, UN monitoring, global education endeavours, publications, and a resource centre.

MADRE, 121 West 27th Street, #301 New York, NY 10001, USA.
Tel: +1 (0)212 627 0444; fax: +1 (0)212 675 3704
E-mail: madre@igc.org
Website: www.madre.org
MADRE is an international women's human rights organisation which develops partnerships with community-based women's organisations which respond to women's immediate needs and work towards the long-term development and political empowerment of women.

Sisterhood is Global Institute (SIGI), 1200 Atwater Avenue, Suite 2, Montréal, Québec, H3Z 1X4, Canada.
Tel: +1 (0)514 846 9366; fax: +1 (0)514 846 9066
Established in 1984, SIGI seeks to deepen the understanding of women's human rights at local, national, regional, and global levels, and to strengthen the capacity of women to exercise their rights through leadership training. It has members in 70 countries, and currently maintains a network of over 1,300 individuals and organisations.

Akina Mama wa Africa, 334-336 Goswell Road, London EC1V 7LQ, UK.
Tel: +44 (020) 7713 5166; fax: +44 (020) 7713 1959; e-mail: gracia@imul.com
Website: www.akinamama.com
'Akina Mama wa Africa' (AMwA) is Swahili for 'solidarity among African women'. AMwA is a non-government development agency set up in 1985 by women from different parts of Africa residing in the UK to create a space for African women to organise autonomously, identify issues of concern to them, and speak for themselves. AMwA aims to provide solidarity, promote awareness, and to build links with African women active in their own development. In 1996 AmwA started the African Women's Leadership Institute in Kampala.

Women in the Media Initiatives, UNESCO, 7, place de Fontenoy, 75352 PARIS 07 SP, France. Tel: +33 (0)1 4568 1000.
Website: www.unesco.org/webworld/com_media/society_women.html
Recognizing the lack of women in the media who can influence content, policies, and access to the means of expression, UNESCO has several initiatives to promote women's participation and representation in the media. UNESCO's tools include the Toronto Platform for Action, the WomMed/FemMed Network (see below), and programmes for training Mediterranean women journalists, and women television producers in the Pacific region.

WomMed/FemMed Network
E-mail: womed@unesco.org
Website: www.unesco.org/webworld/com/wommed_femmed.htm
The WomMed/FemMed Network brings together women and men from around the world who seek to redress the gender imbalance in access to expression and decision-making in the media, reaffirming the importance of pluralistic communication to ensure women's full participation in society, and promoting all forms of democratic communication.

The Network was created by the participants of the UNESCO International Symposium 'Women and the Media: Access to Expression and Decision-making' in Toronto in 1995.

Mujer/Fempress, Casilla 16637, Correo 9, Santiago, Chile. Fax +56 (0)2 2333 996
E-mail: fempress@reuna.cl
Website: www.fempress.org
Fempress was created in 1981 as an information and communication network with the key goals of developing a communication strategy that promotes women's movements and spreading awareness of women's issues through the press and radio. Fempress distributes a monthly magazine and radio programme throughout Latin America.

Mother's Voices,165 West 46th Street, Suite 701, New York, NY 10036, USA.
Tel: +1 (0)212 730 2777
Fax: +1 (0)212 730 4378
Website: www.mvoices.org
Mother's voices is an organisation based in the United States which aims to bring an end to HIV/AIDS around the world. Their mission is to encourage women everywhere to become involved in HIV/AIDS education, improved prevention efforts, fair and effective policy formation, and increased research.

The International Women's Health Coalition (IWHC), 24 East 21 Street New York, NY 10010, USA.
Website: www.iwhc.org
Founded in 1980, the IWHC is a non-profit organisation that works in Africa, Asia, and Latin America to promote women's reproductive and sexual health and rights. IWHC also publishes books and papers, and maintains a global communications network of 6,000 individuals and organisations in 143 countries. In Chile, Nigeria, and Brazil, IWHC supports women's groups that are raising public awareness of HIV/AIDS.

The White Ribbon Campaign: Men Working to End Men's Violence Against Women, 365 Bloor St East, Suite 16000, Toronto, Ontario, M4W 3L4 Canada.
Tel: +1 (0)416 920 6684 or +1 (0)800 328 2228
Fax: +1 (0)416 920 1678
E-mail: whiterib@idirect.com
Website: www.whiteribbon.com.ca
The White Ribbon Campaign (WRC) started out with a handful of men in 1991. Each year the WRC urges men and boys to wear a white ribbon for one to two weeks (25 November- 6 December) as a personal pledge never to commit, condone, or remain silent about violence against women. Their campaign also includes educational work in schools, support of local women's groups, and fundraising for international education efforts.

Men For Change, Box 33005, Quinpool Postal Outlet, Halifax, Nova Scotia, B3L 4T6, Canada. Tel: +1 (0)902 492 4104
E-mail: aa116@chebucto.ns.ca
Website: www.chebucto.ns.ca/Community Support/Men4Change/m4c_back.html
Men for Change was formed in 1989 in response to the killing of women engineering students in Montreal whose murderer singled them out because they were 'feminists'. The group meets regularly to explore male dominance and violence in male-female relationships. Small group meetings offer men the opportunity to share their feelings and reflections on their relationships and identities. While this group's activities are limited to Montreal, Men for Change could serve as a model for men's groups around the world.

International Lesbian and Gay Association (ILGA), 81 Kolenmarkt, B 1000, Brussels, Belgium. Tel/fax: +32 (0)2 502 2471
E-mail: ilga@ilga.org
Website: www.ilga.org
This worldwide federation of national and local groups is dedicated to achieving equal rights for lesbians, gay men, bisexuals, and

transgendered people everywhere. Founded in 1978, it now has more than 350 member organisations from every continent.

United Lesbians of African Heritage (ULOAH), 1626 N. Wilcox Ave, #190, Los Angeles, CA 90028, USA.
Tel +1 (0)323 960 5051
Website: members.aol.com/uloah/home.html
ULOAH host annual retreats and a monthly 'rap group' to discuss issues of importance to lesbian women.

Khuli Zaban (The South Asian/Middle Eastern Lesbian, Bisexual and Transgender Women's Organisation), c/o Shamakami, Inc., PO Box 1006, Jamaica Plain, MA 02130, USA.
Website: www.geocities.com/ WestHollywood/9993/khulizaban.html
Khuli Zaban was formed by a small group of women in 1995. Its website explains that 'creating a space where we are understood, safe, and grounded has been life changing experience for many of the women in khuli zaban'.

Web resources

WomenWatch: The UN Internet Gateway on the Advancement and Empowerment of Women
www.un.org/womenwatch
This website contains links to all UN organisations and inter-government and treaty bodies that work for women's empowerment and gender equality, as well as regional plans of actions from around the globe.

UNIFEM (United Nations Development Fund for Women)
www.unifem.undp.org
UNIFEM's mission is to promote women's empowerment and gender equality. It acts as a catalyst within the UN system, supporting efforts that link the needs and concerns of women to all critical issues on national, regional, and global agendas. Its website has

links to its magazine, Currents, its biennial report, and press releases, as well as to other feminist websites and publications.

Feminist Activist Resources on the Net
www.igc.apc.org/women/feminist.html
This site guides activist feminists to resources on the internet. It lists inks to other websites that explore issues such as reproductive rights, sexual harassment and rape, domestic violence, women of colour, women and politics, women and economic issues, women and health, and women's organisations.

The Electra Pages
http://electrapages.com
The Electra Pages is an on-line database of more than 9,000 women's organisations. Its browser allows you to search for organisations by location, category, and name. It also allows users to add their own listings and correct current listings.

Women Leaders Online/Women Organising for Change
www.wlo.org
This website attempts to empower women in politics, media, society, the economy, and cyberspace.

AVIVA
www.aviva.org
AVIVA is an internet magazine or 'webzine' that women from around the world can contribute to. Run by an international group of women based in London, it also provides free monthly listings of women's groups and events worldwide.

Lesbian.org
www.lesbian.org
One of the earliest and most comprehensive resources for promoting lesbian visibility on the internet, this site contains links related to topics including politics and activism, arts and culture, and lesbian and gay studies.

Matricies, A Lesbian and Lesbian Feminist Research and Network Newsletter, 92 Ford Hall University of Minnesota, Minneapolis, MN 55455, USA.
www.lesbian.org/matrices/index.htm
Matricies is a project of the Centre for Advanced Feminist Studies at the University of Minnesota, which endeavours to increase communication and networking among those interested in lesbian scholarship. Special features include interviews with lesbian scholars, current bibliographies on lesbian topics, book reviews, dissertation abstracts, calls for papers, conference announcements, reports from lesbian research centres, and news and information from lesbian websites.

FeminiStcom
http://feminist.com/
A website with weekly news updates, information on female-owned businesses, a 'bookstore', and a great variety of links to other feminist organisations.

WWWomen.com: Lesbians/Advocacy
www.wwwomen.com/category/lesbia/advoca2.html
This site, hosted by WWWomen.com, has short descriptions of and links to various organisations of lesbian women, including regional chapters of the Lesbian Avengers, the Lesbian Herstory Project, and support groups for lesbian mothers.

'Challenging Dominant Models of Sexuality in Development',seminar series, Institute of Development Studies, University of Brighton, UK.
www.ids.ac.uk
This website makes available papers and summaries of discussions from this January-March 2000 seminar series.

Cultural theory
http://theory.org.uk
Offers further information on cultural theory, including essays on Butler, Foucault, and others.

E-mail lists

GREAT Network is a UK-based organisation based at the School of Development Studies at the University of East Anglia. It disseminates research results to development agencies and academics, informs subscribers of relevant debates and information on the world-wide web, manages topical debates, keeps members up-to-date with job advertisements, and journal and conference calls. To subscribe, send an e-mail stating 'join development-gender [first name last name]' (inserting your first name and last name into the command) to development-gender@mailbase.ac.uk

PROFEM is an internet mailing list that focuses on men, masculitities, and gender relations. It aims to promote dialogue between men and women concerned with gender justice and the elimination of sexism. Additionally, it circulates information relating to research, new initiatives, and resources. To subscribe, send the message 'subscribe profem-1' to majordomo@coombs.edu.au

Video

Macho, by Lucinda Broadbent
(running time 26 mins)
For copies on videotape contact: Lucinda Broadbent, 345 Renfrew St, Glasgow G3 6UW, Scotland. Tel:/Fax: +44 (0)141 332 2042, E-mail: Lucinda@cqm.co.uk
Documents the work of the Nicaraguan group Men Against Violence which aims to combat *machismo* and male violence. Xavier Munos, a member of the group, is personally torn by the sex scandal surrounding his former hero, Daniel Ortega. This lively, engaging, and revealing film follows Xavier on a trip to San Francisco to share cutting-edge techniques to deal with violent men and *macho* behaviour. The video was shot in Managua, Nicaragua, and San Francisco, and the USA. Available in Spanish or with English subtitles.